Managing Your Thesis or Dissertation

A Workbook for Graduate Students

Laurie Waye, Ph.D.
University of Victoria

Kendall Hunt
publishing company

Cover images © 2010 Shutterstock, Inc.

Kendall Hunt
publishing company

www.kendallhunt.com
Send all inquiries to:
4050 Westmark Drive
Dubuque, IA 52004-1840

Copyright © 2011 by Kendall Hunt Publishing Company

ISBN 978-0-7575-8764-1

All rights reserved. No part of this publication may be reproduced, stored in a retrieval system, or transmitted, in any form or by any means, electronic, mechanical, photocopying, recording, or otherwise, without the prior written permission of the copyright owner.

Printed in the United States of America
10 9 8 7 6 5 4 3 2 1

I dedicate this book to all graduate students who are struggling to write their theses, projects, and dissertations. May this workbook help you finish.

Contents

Introduction VII

Step 1: FIND THE BEGINNING 1

So Where Is the Beginning? 2
Building Your Map 2
    Project Management Principle #1: Creating a map 2
Get Going 3
    GRADUATE STUDENT TIP: The literature review as a party 8

Step 2: GET FOCUSED 11

What Can Go? 11
    Project Management Principle #2: Analyzing the scope of the project 11
Get Going 14
Management Skills: A Top Ten List 14
    GRADUATE STUDENT TIP: What a thesis/dissertation *really* is 22

Step 3: IDENTIFY TASKS 25

The Academic Writing Process: 40/20/40 25
    The First 40 25
    The Middle 20 27
    The Final 40 30
    Project Management Principle #3: Identifying the tasks 31
Get Going 32
    GRADUATE STUDENT TIP: Are you a *nouveau* graduate student? 35

Step 4: **ORGANIZE YOUR TASKS** 37
    Project Management Principle #4: Creating the Work Breakdown Structure (WBS) 37
    Project Management Principle #5: Identifying the Critical Path 37
  Get Going 40
    GRADUATE STUDENT TIP: Are you demonstrating academic integrity? 41

Step 5: **MAKE A PLAN** 45
    Project Management Principle #6: The Gantt chart 45
  Get Going 45
    GRADUATE STUDENT TIP: Take Control of Feedback 48

Step 6: **FOLLOW YOUR PLAN** 53
    Project Management Principle #7: Ownership 53
    Project Management Principle #8: Use your resources 54
  Get Going 55
    GRADUATE STUDENT TIP: Self-editing strategies 56

References 67
Appendix 69
  Extra mind map pages 70
  Extra Gantt chart pages 86
  Gee (2001) storyboard 91
  Feedback chart 92
  Self-editing checklist 95

Introduction

Welcome to *Managing Your Thesis or Dissertation*! This workbook will help you organize your thoughts, research, and writing so that you can create the best thesis—which we all know is a *finished* thesis. While this book is intended for graduate students working on their thesis, project, or dissertation, you can use it for any writing project. Grant applications, statements of research intent, and proposals can all be written more efficiently and effectively using the tools in this workbook.

I've used these methods with graduate students I've worked with at the university where I work and I've used them myself. As a PhD student I needed to be organized for a variety of reasons. For the first half of my PhD, I was a single parent. My mornings and evenings were jam-packed with parenting, but my days were scarily free. For the second half of my PhD, I was a mom of one and step-mom of four while working full time. Both scenarios required planning and self-discipline. While graduate students who are as busy as I was in the second half of my studies may feel little pity for those with empty hours during the day, those who have empty hours can crave structure and human interaction. Without such structure you can find yourself scheduling naps and justifying to yourself why you get an hour off to watch *Oprah*.

This workbook was also developed from what I watch graduate students go through. In my role as coordinator of the Writing Centre at the University of Victoria, I've worked with many graduate students who are overwhelmed with the process of writing such a large and complex document. Those who come through the writing centre complain of unhelpful supervisors, conflicting feedback from committee members, a hectic schedule, pressure to produce published articles and present at conferences, a lack of departmental writing support, and a whole host of other things. This doesn't mean that graduate students are complainers; it means that they are busy people being asked to do a number of things, including researching articles, reading them, writing about them, planning their own research based on their understanding of them, and then writing about this research. A graduate student's life is, indeed, very full, and even fuller if you have children, a spouse, a job, health issues, and/or other commitments. Add to this list the need for exercise, sleep, a balanced diet, and a steady job once that thesis is finished, and you're likely as stressed out as I was as a graduate student and as the graduate students I work with.

Some would argue that stress is a natural part of being a student. In some ways this is true. I don't believe, however, that things should be more stressful than they need to be. Writing a thesis is stressful because you have a tough audience to please and you're probably new to the format and expectations of a thesis. However, the stress of how to get it done doesn't need to eat away at you. By following the principles in this book you can reduce the amount of stress that the thesis creates for you. It's like climbing a mountain: If you focus on the summit—the finished thesis—then it becomes hard to even put one foot in front of the other. If you create a map to help you climb the mountain—which this workbook will help you do—then you can stop paying attention to the summit and start focusing on what you need to do today to get that thesis done.

To create this map, I used eight principles of project management. These are the same eight I introduce to students in workshops and tutorials. Project management is an approach to handling large undertakings such as developing a new computer program or building a house. While it isn't a perfect fit for graduate student work, these eight principles are a good match:

1. Drawing out your ideas and their connection to each other in a concept map,
2. Analyzing the scope of the project,
3. Identifying tasks to be done,
4. Creating the Work Breakdown Structure (WBS),
5. Identifying the critical path,
6. Making a Gantt chart to organize the work,
7. Understanding ownership of the project,
8. Using your resources.

By applying these principles of project management, you will learn to break your writing into a to-do list and a timeline that's not only reasonable but also achievable, regardless of writing ability or family and work commitments. These principles are introduced and complemented by:

- A step-by-step guide for developing a writing plan and timeline,
- A workbook section that invites students to make maps and charts to guide and plan their writing,
- Ideas to help balance the many roles graduate students play in addition to student (parent, research assistant, full-time worker, etc.), including tips for time management,
- Suggestions for overcoming procrastination, perfectionism, and over-identification with one's writing, as well as
- A formula to follow again and again when writing a larger piece of work.

While there are computer programs designed to help you organize all of these principles, unless you plan to use project management software in the future then you are better off learning the principles that apply best to you and focus on your thesis. Learning new software can be interesting and rewarding, but it can also be time consuming and procrastination inducing. My recommendation is that you use this workbook, learn these eight principles, and once your thesis is done, decide whether to pursue your interest in project management. If you are truly interested, then post-thesis is a great time to learn more about it.

To get the most out of this workbook, I recommend using coloured pencils or markers and sticky notes. There are extra pages at the back for future projects or if you want to start an activity over again, so don't hesitate to write, draw, and shade without too much thought. You can always make changes later. While you may feel a bit silly at first—after all, it may have been years since you wrote in a colour other than black or blue—you'll soon find that the activities in this book will in fact help you organize better, feel less stress about writing your thesis, and produce more writing.

I wish you the best of luck with your thesis! Breathe deeply, plan thoroughly, and finish that thesis.

Image © Ovchynnikov Oleksii, 2011.
Used under license from Shutterstock, Inc.

Find the Beginning

STEP 1

Being a graduate student takes a lot of dedication, time, and effort. More than that, it requires a kind of tenacity to be dedicated, put in the time, and make the effort for the duration of your studies. By the time you get to writing your thesis, project, or dissertation, you may be tired and feel overwhelmed. Or, you may get stuck midway through the thesis. Either way, you may need some organizational and motivational support. The principles introduced here will provide the organizational support by helping you discern what you need to do, when you need to do it, and how you are going to do it. The motivational support comes from the advice given in this book and from achieving your daily thesis goals. It might help to know that your struggles are common and that there are ways to overcome them. Please note that for the sake of simplicity, I have used *thesis* in this workbook as a catch-all term for thesis, project, and dissertation.

While graduate students are necessarily smart people and good at reading, it can be helpful to have examples that demonstrate what you are being asked to do. For this reason I have included in this book two hypothetical graduate students. After a few years out in the workforce, Jiro is in the Faculty of Education to do his PhD. He's still completing his coursework but is already thinking about his dissertation. Jiro is also a single parent and works part-time. His plan is to become a tenure-track instructor at a university. The other student is Maria; she's in the Faculty of Science to do her MSc in Biology. She has completed her coursework and is now writing her thesis. She doesn't work, which she finds isolating. In addition, English is her second language. Her goal is to get a non-academic job, such as a lab instructor at the university or as a research scientist for the government. Throughout this book you will see examples of how Maria and Jiro use the tools described in this book to organize their thesis writing.

So Where Is the Beginning?

No matter where you are in your writing, taking stock of what you know about your writing project helps you make an overall plan. Not having a plan is rather like not having a map. As I said in the introduction, without a map, the mountain you are about to climb can seem daunting. With a map, you can focus on the path directly ahead of you, trusting that you will reach the peak because your map is well made and familiar—after all, you wrote it! If you can find out what those small steps are and in which order they should be taken, then you are on your way to climbing the mountain of your thesis. Don't look at the peak; keep your eyes on the trail.

Take the time now to create your map by using the project management tools and the advice in this workbook. Once created, you can focus on the handful of things you need to do today to complete your thesis in the near future. Knowing you have a plan and that your plan will work for you should ease some of the graduate student stress.

Building Your Map

Project Management Principle #1: Creating a map

There are a few names for the kind of map I'm going to ask you to do here: *concept map* or *mind map* are two of the more common ones. In this book I refer to them as mind maps because the one you will make in this chapter will contain concepts, references to literature you have read, questions you have, and so on. You are going to take what's in your mind and put it on paper so you can organize it. As a thesis writer, you need to (a) take stock of where you are at so you can figure out where to go next and (b) ascertain that the route you are taking is the quickest and least painful.

This workbook is designed to show you how to implement each project management principle; there are places for you to apply the principle to your own work. Use the included worksheets for this to get an idea of what you are doing. If you feel comfortable and confident with mind mapping, I suggest investing in some large paper and markers or pencil crayons.

Large paper, such as newspaper rolls, allows you to write bigger and to include more information because you control the length of the paper. You can post your mind map on the wall by your desk or carry it folded in your backpack or bag. A portable mind map means you can easily add information and ideas in any location. Carrying a mind map is a great idea if you are still engaged in the "thinking and exploring" stage of your research and writing.

If portability isn't important to you, and the people you live with don't mind, try using washable markers to create your mind map on a window or a sliding glass door. Working while standing, such as when you are adding to your mind map on the wall or window, will give your body a break from sitting. Being a graduate student means a whole lot of hunching over a desk and a keyboard; seize the opportunity to create a more dynamic workspace for yourself.

Whether you use the templates in this workbook, large paper from a roll, or the window above your desk, I highly recommend using colour to create your mind map. Not only is colour fun to use—and as adults we often don't have enough time to play with colour—but it can help you group themes and items more easily. As you start your mind map, try playing with colour. Some students I have worked with when teaching them how to use these principles disliked using colour: They said they felt childish. With encouragement, though, all of them found that by using at least two colours, they were able to organize their mind map in a way that was very meaningful to them.

Get Going

Look at the following pages. In the circle in the middle of pages 6 and 7, write where you are now. Think about this for a few minutes because if your map locates you in a different starting point than where you really are at, you might end up having to redo it. Some ideas of what you might want to put in that circle:

- An overview of your thesis
- Key words of what your study is about
- Your research question(s)
- The title of the chapter you are currently writing

You may also want to put in that circle the issue that's currently plaguing your writing, such as a loss of passion for the topic, difficulties with your supervisor, or time management challenges. If you decide to focus on what's keeping you from finishing your thesis, then be sure to adjust the activities in this workbook to focus on that. Planning your writing won't help you much if you really need to figure out how to get writing. Once you have a plan in place for dealing with that particular issue, or set of issues, then you can use the extra worksheets provided to plan your writing.

When you are ready, move on to the next step. From the middle circle, draw nodes branching out. Most students will have between two and five nodes stemming from the middle circle. Give a title to each node. These nodes might represent, for example, your literature review, your methodology, and your discussion section. Or, the nodes might represent a refinement of the key words you wrote in the circle. This is a particularly helpful strategy if you are still trying to narrow your topic or decide which smaller segment of your area of interest to focus on. In this case you will write narrower segments or aspects of the main topic of study.

Jiro's Mind Map

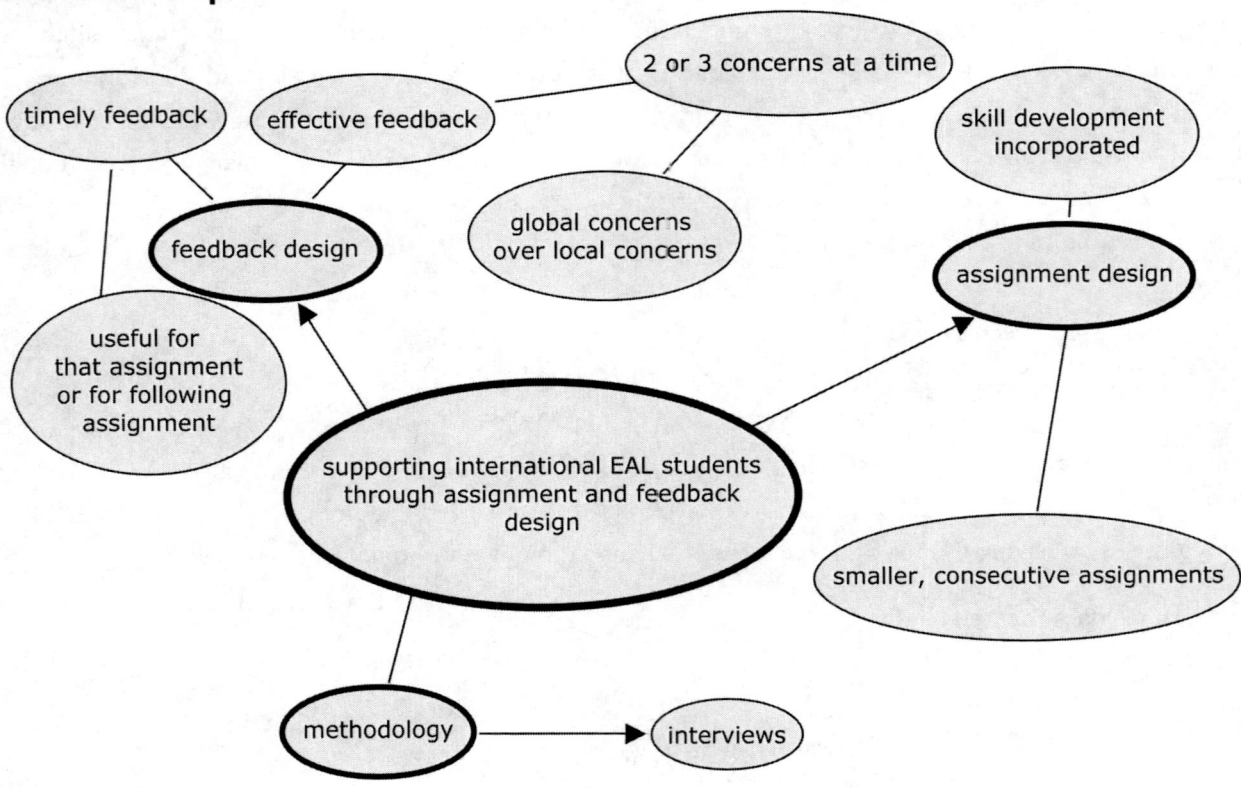

- timely feedback
- effective feedback
- 2 or 3 concerns at a time
- skill development incorporated
- feedback design
- global concerns over local concerns
- assignment design
- useful for that assignment or for following assignment
- **supporting international EAL students through assignment and feedback design**
- smaller, consecutive assignments
- methodology → interviews

As you can see, you are taking what's in the circle and breaking it down into its component parts. The goal of this activity is to take all of those thoughts and pieces of knowledge in your mind and put them down on paper. From each node you will add more nodes, branching off to add even more detail to your mind map. Nodes you might want to add:

- Relevant research you have read
- The "big names" in your field
- Goals of your research

You might like to experiment using a sticky note for each node. This is a useful technique because you can later move the nodes around if you decide on different groupings. Colour is also useful because you can use it to denote connections, themes, and groupings. In addition to being useful, you may just find it fun. (I used sticky notes for my thesis only once because my then–three-year-old rearranged them the first chance he got.)

While you are creating your mind map, look at the boxes in the bottom two corners of the page. One is labeled "The Worry Box" and the other "The Question Box." In the Worry Box you write your worries, fears, and doubts. For example, this is where you would write that nagging question of whether or not you can finish your thesis by the deadline, or if you will be able to find a job after you have finished graduate school. The worries could also be more immediate, such as if you will be able to even find time to write your thesis, or whether you will be able to recruit enough participants for your study. Money concerns, family issues, and your physical health are other worries to note if they pop into your mind while creating your mind map. Worries, fears, and

Maria's Mind Map

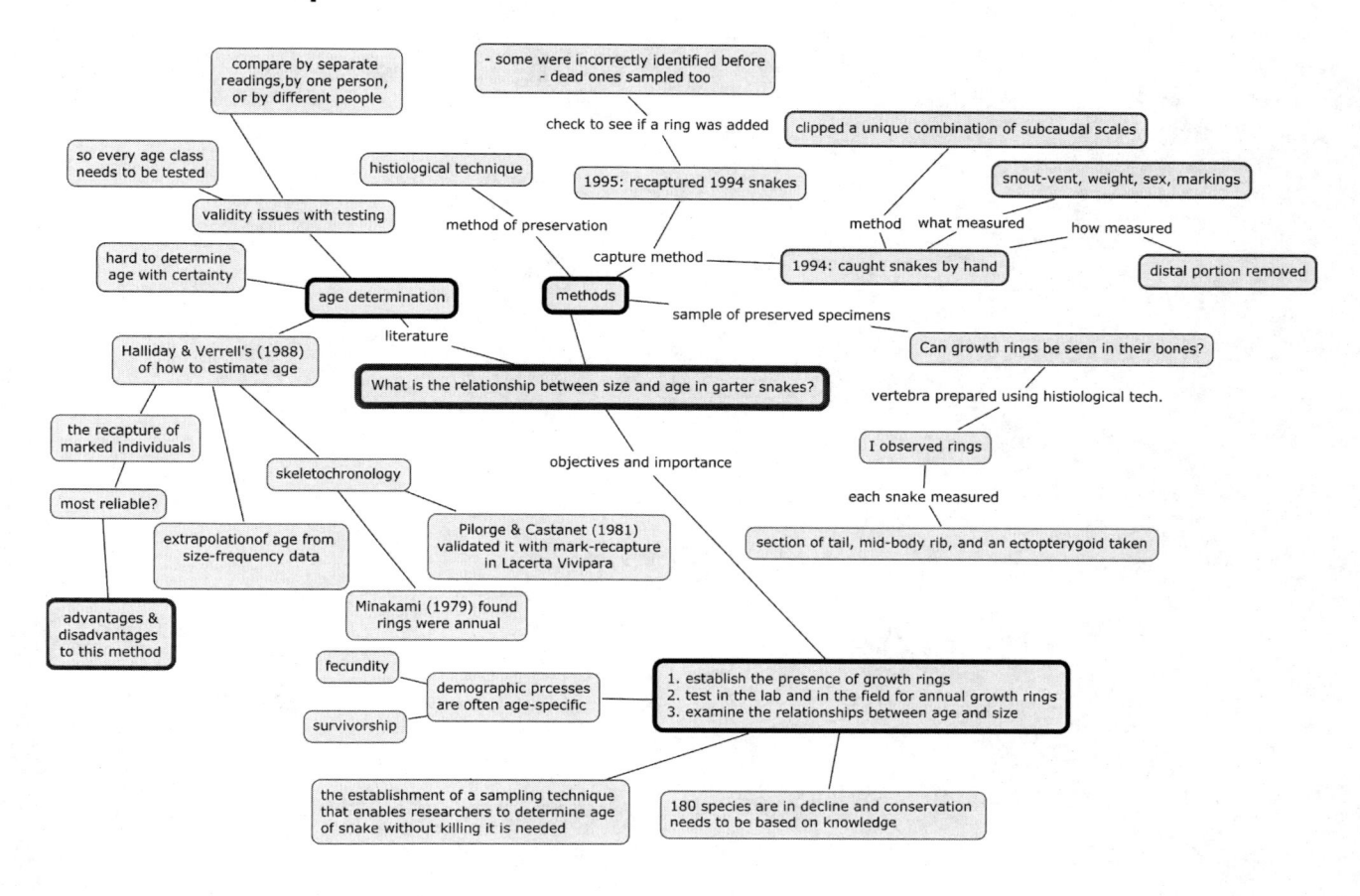

[Mind map diagram with central question "What is the relationship between size and age in garter snakes?" branching into:]

age determination branch:
- hard to determine age with certainty
- validity issues with testing — so every age class needs to be tested
- compare by separate readings, by one person, or by different people
- histological technique
- Halliday & Verrell's (1988) of how to estimate age
  - the recapture of marked individuals — most reliable?
  - skeletochronology
    - Pilorge & Castanet (1981) validated it with mark-recapture in Lacerta Vivipara
    - Minakami (1979) found rings were annual
  - extrapolation of age from size-frequency data
  - advantages & disadvantages to this method

methods branch:
- check to see if a ring was added — 1995: recaptured 1994 snakes
  - some were incorrectly identified before
  - dead ones sampled too
- capture method — 1994: caught snakes by hand
  - method: clipped a unique combination of subcaudal scales
  - what measured: snout-vent, weight, sex, markings
  - how measured: distal portion removed
- method of preservation
- sample of preserved specimens — Can growth rings be seen in their bones?
  - vertebra prepared using histological tech.
  - I observed rings
  - each snake measured
  - section of tail, mid-body rib, and an ectopterygoid taken

objectives and importance branch:
1. establish the presence of growth rings
2. test in the lab and in the field for annual growth rings
3. examine the relationships between age and size

- demographic processes are often age-specific
  - fecundity
  - survivorship
- the establishment of a sampling technique that enables researchers to determine age of snake without killing it is needed
- 180 species are in decline and conservation needs to be based on knowledge

---

doubts don't need to interfere with your work, but they do need to be acknowledged. Putting them in their own special place lets you feel these concerns and reminds you to look at them and consider them later.

The Question Box is where you put all the questions that arise while making your mind map. You may write something like "How long is a proposal in my discipline?" or "Is it possible to defend my dissertation by the end of the year?" These are questions you will ask later. Once your map is complete you can revisit these questions to determine of whom you should ask them and when they need to be asked.

Continue adding nodes to your mind map until you feel confident that all that was in your mind about your thesis is now down on the paper in front of you.

FINALLY, A PLACE TO PUT MY QUESTIONS AND CONCERNS!

Image © Icons Jewelry, 2011. Used under license from Shutterstock, Inc.

The Worry Box

Step 1: Find the Beginning

The Question Box

Managing Your Thesis or Dissertation

GRADUATE STUDENT TIP:

The literature review as a party

For a while now I have been reading about the kinds of writing that happen in different disciplines. One of the best descriptions I came across was a metaphor about graduate school and the learning curve academic discourse (the way we write, speak, and display knowledge in each discipline) requires. Burke (1967) describes discipline-specific academic discourse as a party:

> You enter, listen to the conversation, add your thoughts, someone else adds to those thoughts, you agree with someone, and someone disagrees with you. Eventually you leave the party and others arrive.

I extend this metaphor to graduate writing so it encompasses the experience of learning to add your voice and thoughts to the conversation that is happening in your discipline. Here's my version of Burke's metaphor:

> You enter a party, late. You don't know anyone, but they are engaged in a heated debate. You can't enter the discussion until you have listened long enough to know who has said what, and who is agreeing with whom. The issues become clearer the more you listen, and you learn the names of the people that most of the party-goers are listening to. Eventually you build up enough contextual and background knowledge to add your own ideas to the conversation, but not before you understand how to appropriately add your ideas.

As a graduate student, you enter the party of academia as a latecomer. Take solace in knowing that all graduate students enter late. You can also take solace in knowing that after you have left the party, more newcomers will arrive and be as equally surprised by how people talk about the research and theories in the field.

Step 1: Find the Beginning

Writing a literature review is like writing a review of a party. Who was there, who said what, and who agreed with whom informs the reader of the context in which your research and thesis occur.

If you'd like some pointers on how to talk about what others said or wrote, check out the templates at the end of the great little book, *They Say, I Say,* by Gerald Graff and Cathy Birkenstein (2006).

Image © brushingup, 2011. Used under license from Shutterstock, Inc.

Get Focused

Once your mind map is complete, take a look at it. Imagine yourself taking a physical step back from it to look at it objectively. What's missing? Which nodes are less developed and what can you add to flesh them out?

If you think you may need to redo your mind map to put something else in the centre—for example, a specific node you want to work on next or a different aspect of your topic—make another mind map with the extra pages provided in the Appendix. Once you are satisfied with your mind map, you are ready to move on.

What Can Go?

Project Management Principle #2: Analyzing the scope of the project

The second project management principle we use is analyzing the contents of the mind map to determine if you can realistically do all that you've outlined. After all, it's far easier to write well on a narrow topic than a broad one. If your topic is narrow, then you can explore its aspects deeply. If your topic is too broad, then you will be able to talk about its aspects only in a more shallow manner. While theses used to have hundreds of pages, the trend these days is toward shorter, more concise, and tightly focused documents.

If your project is too broad, it may be because you haven't decided exactly what you want to focus on. Having lots of ideas is usually great, but when it comes time to write your proposal or your comprehensive exams, you need to have chosen one specific topic. This may mean that one of the topics you're passionate about needs to be put aside until you are done with your thesis. The thesis shouldn't be the last thing you write, so it doesn't need to include everything you are interested in about your topic.

Likewise, your thesis doesn't need to include everything you've written on your mind map. Take a look at your mind map to determine what parts can go. What are your limitations in terms of time and money? If you'd like to be a graduate student for a very long time, you may want to tackle as large a topic as possible. If you'd like to finish graduate school in a timely manner and with less debt and time spent out of the workforce, you may want to restrict the scope of your thesis so you can get it done. Another aspect is if you have funding to do the research. How much can you realistically accomplish with the money you have? Try asking yourself:

- What might make a good follow-up study? That's the sort of thing you will want to put in your discussion or limitations section.
- What might be better addressed as a limitation of your study, rather than incorporated into your study? For example, it's okay to say that your study could have been better if you compared your results by asking the same questions by survey and to focus groups. It may be that due to time and funding restrictions, you can only do the focus groups. That's a limitation, and believe me, you want to think of all the limitations to your study before your external examiner does.
- What might be a natural second part of your study that would be too overwhelming to do for a master's thesis but would make a good thing to write about in your doctoral application, or for a doctoral student, for postdoc studies? Demonstrate that you know how your study fits into the existing literature and where it can lead in future research.

Just as all projects in the business world need to be assessed for their scope—Is it doable? If not, what can go?—as a graduate student you need to assess your mind map as objectively as you can. What can go? And how can you turn that pruning to your advantage?

Let's look at Jiro's mind map. As you can see, it's pretty vague and far-reaching, which reflects the early stage he's at in thinking about his thesis.

Jiro's Example of Scope

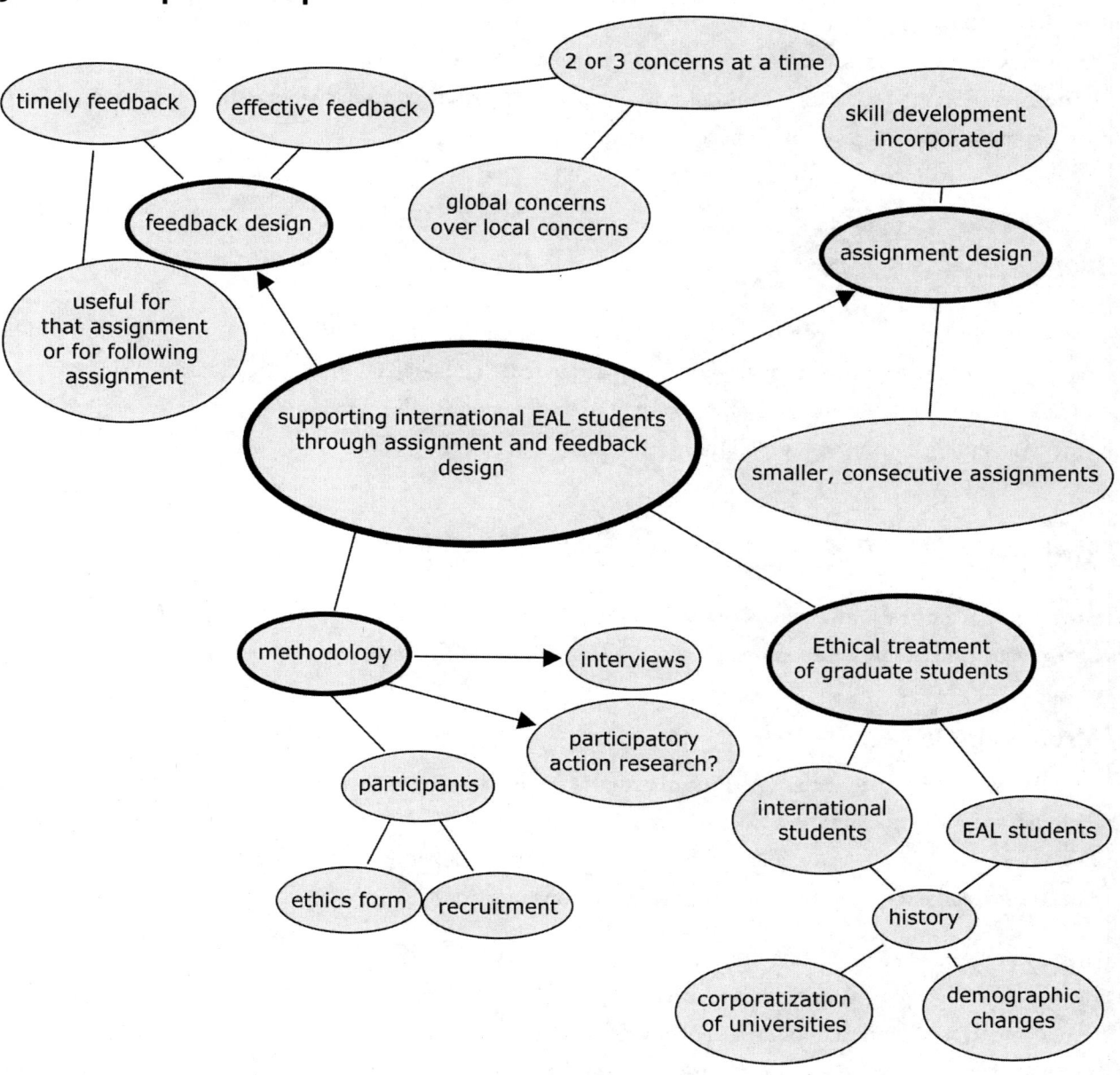

[Mind map diagram with central node "supporting international EAL students through assignment and feedback design" connected to:]

- **feedback design** (bold node)
  - timely feedback
  - effective feedback
    - 2 or 3 concerns at a time
  - global concerns over local concerns
  - useful for that assignment or for following assignment
- **assignment design** (bold node)
  - skill development incorporated
  - smaller, consecutive assignments
- **methodology** (bold node)
  - interviews
  - participatory action research?
  - participants
    - ethics form
    - recruitment
- **Ethical treatment of graduate students** (bold node)
  - international students
  - EAL students
  - history
    - corporatization of universities
    - demographic changes

By looking at his mind map, Jiro can see that he's trying to undertake too much in his proposal. This is especially important because he's still unsure of the exact details of his study. The easiest part to cut is the node on the ethical treatment of students. He will cut out part of his mind map to include that in another project or in the limitations section of his thesis.

While he may initially worry that he won't have enough to write about, this is almost never the case. As I mentioned before, a great piece of writing advice is to choose a topic that's narrow so that you can explore it deeply. A broad topic is like those dreaded first-year courses from your undergrad days: long and shallow and uninteresting. It's hard to say anything new if you can't talk about something in depth. A narrow topic lets you do that.

Managing Your Thesis or Dissertation

If you've made your mind map about an issue, such as rekindling your passion for your topic, then this stage may not apply to you in the same way. Instead, your mind map should provide you with a good description of the various aspects of your issue. You might want to analyze your mind map to find what aspects of your issue can be dealt with sooner and which can wait until later. When you are considering an issue you need to address, finding a starting point to resolving it becomes most important.

GET GOING

Look at your mind map. Is there a piece that can be cut out and used strategically later? Is it possible for you to complete the entire project within your desired timeframe? Be realistic and pragmatic. Your goal should be to undertake a thorough description of your research: no more, no less. Think focused and concise, not rambling and epic. You simply can't cover everything.

MANAGEMENT SKILLS: A TOP TEN LIST

Just as it's important to know what doesn't need to be a part of your thesis, it's important to know how to maximize your time, energy, and effort. Here's my Top Ten list of things you may want to try.

1. Write like it's your job.

Getting down to writing your thesis—I mean actually typing words onto a blank document—can be difficult. Try thinking of writing your thesis like it's your job and you are being paid to do it. In a way you are being paid to write your thesis, because you are, in effect, writing your ticket out of graduate school and into the job market. To write like it's your job, put writing first in your priorities.

In addition, thinking of writing like it's your job can help you distance yourself from negative emotions you may experience regarding your thesis, supervisor, or graduate program. Some students are fortunate enough to have a smooth graduate school experience with a great supervisor, a well-structured program, and support with their writing. Others have a rocky, emotional, and frustrating experience. If you are one of the latter, you may need to try separating your emotions and frustration from what you are writing. Train yourself to think that completing the thesis is a job, and that job is composed of smaller tasks. The tasks are work to be done. By knowing what you need to do, how you are going to do it, and when, as described in the following steps of this workbook, you can practice creating some emotional distance between your work and the rough experience you are having.

2. Schedule your day.

This idea builds on the first suggestion: Know what you have to do, make what you have to do a priority, and figure out how your day will be structured around your priority. One of the less successful ways to write is to try to do it all at once. If you try to write in, say, a three-hour block of time, then you will likely get caught up in a loop of rereading what you have already written (which is a no-no in thesis writing unless you are at the end of a section), struggle with a form of writer's block because your brain can't maintain the momentum of writing for three hours straight, or create fanciful tangents that will later need to be edited out.

Your day should have a variety of tasks in it. If you work full-time, you'll need to determine which two or three tasks you can do outside of work and if you can squeeze one task in during the workday at lunchtime. If you are lucky enough that your studies are your job, maintaining productivity and focus may be issues for you. Schedule your whole day and reframe your studies as your job.

Forty-five to ninety minutes should be your longest task in order to maintain maximum concentration. Try to balance writing tasks with reading and sitting tasks with jobs that allow you to move around. The body wasn't meant to sit for hours on end, nor was the brain designed to think deeply for an extended time. Some activities let us use different parts of our bodies and our brains: Put your mind map on the wall or on a sliding door so you have to stand up to look at it or add to it. Use newspaper roll on the floor to map out the details of each section before you write it. If you are editing as part of your tasks, put up the pages of your section on a string with clothes pegs and hang it across your room.

Image © 3DDock, 2011. Used under license from Shutterstock, Inc.

With a cup of coffee or tea in hand, you can browse your writing and assess if the order of the section is indeed the most logical. You can simply change the order of the paper elements and see what you think.

As you try to create a balance of tasks in your day, try to balance yourself as well. An enjoyable chat with old friends can rejuvenate you. Some time at the gym will keep your energy levels high. Cooking good food will feed not only your body but your mind, as well. Your tasks should be varied, allowing you to move between those that require intense concentration and those that release the tension of that concentration. Remember, it's not the amount of time you put in that's important; it's the quality of the time you put in.

③ Mornings are better than evenings for writing.

You may not be happy to read this, but mornings are better times to write than evenings. There are two reasons why. One, what you do first thing in the morning gets done more often than the things you plan to do later in the day. What you want to get done tomorrow, then, you should plan to do first thing tomorrow morning.

In addition, break larger, important tasks into smaller ones and spread them throughout the day. Why? Saving your work for one particular chunk of time is risky because if you can't get to it, that's three hours of work you had planned to do that won't get done. That puts you behind schedule by a significant amount.

The point is that breaking up your work during the day means you are more likely to get some of it, if not all of it, done. Think of all things that might happen to derail your planned study session: a computer crash, a sick pet, a family emergency. I'm not saying that these things are less likely to happen if you spread out your thesis work during the day; I'm saying that these things will affect your overall progress less. If you break up your time, you may get just one or two writing sessions done in a day, but that's better than none at all.

Managing Your Thesis or Dissertation

Of course the really big things in life—illness, family matters, and financial stress—require our attention and may slow our progress. However, we are more likely to keep going, albeit at a reduced rate, if we can take on a little chunk at a time. If that little chunk gets attended to first thing in the morning, then it'll probably get done, whereas if you leave it to the evening, it's less likely to get done.

The second reason to write first thing in the morning is that for some people the quality of their writing is better at that time. That makes it worth trying, because not only will you get a chunk of writing done before the day has really started, but it may be the best chunk you write all day. The reason? Your brain is still really only able to focus on so much, so you have fewer distractions and your focus is only on the task at hand. I should note that "early morning writing" can occur at noon, if that's first thing in the day for you.

To help you maximize early-morning writing, set up your coffee maker or teapot the night before. You should also write a note to yourself (I use a sticky note on my laptop) to remind yourself what you're writing the next morning. Make a goal that's achievable within the forty-five to ninety-minute time frame. Gather any materials you will need to write that section, such as journal articles or your research journal. When you wake up, turn on your preferred caffeine-preparation device and your computer. Reread your note to yourself, and without rereading what you wrote the previous day, start writing. Don't check e-mail or read the headlines. Turn off the Internet and your cell phone. No one needs you for these forty-five minutes. In addition, you owe it to yourself to accomplish this task.

The last two things you should do before you stop writing is write the first sentence of the next section or paragraph (this creates a smooth transition and makes the next writing session easier to start) and make the next note to remind yourself what you are writing about.

If you are still unconvinced, think about those papers you wrote in your undergraduate days that included that tangent written at 3 a.m. that sunk your paper. Spending too much time writing without the necessary breaks to be objective about where you are going with it and how on track you are can lead to these tangents, and worse: a midnight epiphany that you are writing on the completely wrong topic. Avoid hitting the delete key on all your hard work by treating your writing like a job, working on it in chunks to give you some distance from your writing and your topic, and find times other than at night to do it.

4 Find time in odd places.

So how, then, will you write, if not at night? Take a look at your daily schedule. Some people might find it easier to think about their daily schedule if they mapped it out. Search like a detective for bits of time where you can write, read, or edit. For me, I found that arriving at my son's school thirty minutes before the final bell put me in a place where no one could ask anything of me, I had no Internet access, and I could work in my car for a focused half hour. Creating time by being early for appointments is a great way to carve out bits of time for your work without moving around too many of your other commitments.

Another idea is to shave some time for your work away from another activity. For example, rather than watching your child's swim lesson, you could be studying in the rec centre's café. If you find it hard to study for the whole lesson because you really want to see your child learn to swim, allow yourself half of the lesson to watch and half to work. I do this during my son's soccer lessons. When they are warming up and learning skills, I'm working. When they are playing a game, I'm watching. By dividing this time I accomplish my task and stay engaged in my son's soccer. Every thirty minutes helps! Again, to get the most out of each chunk of time, know what you are going to do in each chunk beforehand and come prepared, whether you need your laptop, your research journal, or a hard copy of the last chapter you wrote that needs editing.

5. Have a regular place to write.

For those who are great at finding reasons to not write, I suggest you create a regular writing place. Do nothing in that place except write your thesis. Have only the books and articles there that will help you write the section you are currently working on. Avoid cluttering the space so you reduce the distractions around you. Train yourself to sit there and write. Three times a day, for forty-five minutes at a time, is a reasonable goal. Remember, you are writing a piece of nonfiction and you already know what it's going to be about. You only need to write it. The muse of inspiration doesn't need to visit you. You don't need to be in the mood to write. It's just another task on your to-do list.

Yes, I've been accused of sucking the beauty and inspiration out of writing. The truth is that I do this intentionally. Many students have been led to believe that writing is a tortured, inspired, and beautiful undertaking. It certainly can be, but academic writing requires a clear head, determination, and careful planning. When you are revising your writing (discussed later in this workbook) you can take the time to make your sentences beautiful, your transitions smooth, and your metaphors witty.

As for inspiration, I believe that comes mainly in the stage when you plan your writing (discussed in the next chapter). You may be inspired by the articles you've read, by your supervisor, and by the university environment. Life experiences and interests can also fuel the passion for your topic. Through this inspiration come the ideas, which get organized and ordered. When engaged in academic writing, you're telling the audience what you read, what you did, and what you thought. You've already been inspired, so there's no need for more inspiration to narrate what has already happened.

6. Procrastinate effectively.

This oxymoron is actually possible if you're aware of what you are doing. Let's start by describing what is *ineffective* procrastination. You know you should get down to work, but you end up organizing your sock drawer by colour, writing a bunch of e-mails, or watching YouTube videos for an hour. During that time you have that nagging voice inside your mind telling you to focus on what really needs to get done. You ignore that voice to the best of your abilities, but feel a little bit bad about it. This is ineffective procrastination because you are simply avoiding work. It's of little, if any, benefit to you.

Effective procrastination is different. You know you need to get down to work, but you have doubts about the next section you're going to write or some questions you want to mull over after reading that last article.

Instead of forcing yourself to do something you were supposed to do but aren't mentally prepared to do, you go organize your sock drawer by colour or go for a walk. While engaged in this activity, you think about that next section or those questions that article raised for you. When you have finished your effective-procrastination activity at a set time, you get back to work. Here's what makes this form of "procrastination" effective:

- You're spending the time away from work actually working—thinking is, after all, a great part of graduate school.
- The amount of time you spend doing the other activity is predetermined.
- The activity you engage in allows you to think.
- When doing the procrastination activity, your thoughts are focused on what's keeping you physically away from your work.
- You feel justified in stepping away from your work to think something through.

7 Be periodically disconnected.

You don't need to be available by e-mail, text messaging, and social network sites all the time. In fact, these communication tools can be the very things that dismantle your work plan and disrupt your train of thought. When you are working, whether it be writing, reading, or thinking, allow yourself to be disconnected. You are setting yourself up for success when you do what you can to foster your focus and promote your effectiveness.

If people worry that they can't get hold of you during that hour, then perhaps you need to indicate to them what you are doing and why. Have a system whereby they can reach you in the case of a true emergency, but be sure to define what constitutes an emergency. Instead of resenting your temporary disconnection, your friends and family will likely respect your decision and come to admire it.

Likewise, set parameters for yourself regarding e-mail and social networking sites. Effective workers will tell you that they check e-mail at certain times during the day and otherwise get on with their other tasks. For example, three times a day is plenty of connection time. While you may not believe me, experiment with this and see how much you're actually missing out on and how much more work you accomplish. Checking and responding to e-mails regularly instead of constantly will improve your productivity and move you that much closer to completing your thesis.

Image © Icons Jewelry, 2011. Used under license from Shutterstock, Inc.

8 Put perfectionism on hold.

Perfectionism has its good points: at best, it forces you to work hard and to hold yourself to high standards. At worst, it paralyzes you. If you're paralyzed in your work, ask yourself if there is actually something else going on. If you're afraid of failing, then you might need to talk to your supervisor, a counselor, or your graduate advisor about that. You may be suffering from the "Cinderella Syndrome:" You are at the ball (i.e., graduate school) but you don't really belong there. You're worried about being found out for who you really are. Well, the good news is that many graduate students feel that this particular glass slipper fits them; it's easy to feel uncomfortable and unprepared in graduate school. You were accepted into the program on your own merit and you'll succeed on your own merit.

If you find yourself being a perfectionist about your writing, ask yourself if you actually are trying to procrastinate. If so, spend some time thinking about why you are procrastinating. What's bugging you? What's preventing you from getting down to work? Once you have pinpointed the cause of your procrastination you can begin to address it.

It's worth determining where your perfectionism comes from, because its effects can be stifling. In addition to paralysis, it can cause a self-created writer's block. You can't write because you won't let yourself write badly—which is exactly what you need to do in a draft since you trust yourself to revise well later on. Another issue may be that you are editing too soon. Instead of writing more each time you sit, you go over the same section, improving it each time but never writing what comes next. Don't interfere with your own writing and progress.

⑨ Use people-management skills.

Regardless of the discipline you're in, you have to communicate with people. You need things from your committee members and supervisor, like feedback and advice. If you don't have a great sense of people-management skills, I suggest you use your thesis as a way to develop them. You're going to need them after your degree, as well, whether you end up in academia or not. If you feel you could use some pointers, I suggest the classic *How to Win Friends and Influence People,* by Dale Carnegie (1981 revised version).

With your now-stunning people-management skills, which include respecting people's time, asking nicely, and focusing on win–win situations, identify the conversations you need to have. What do you need from your supervisor? Your committee members? Think more broadly, too. Is your office mate driving you crazy with his incessant peanut-shell cracking? Does your partner understand your need to study? Do you need to ask family members to babysit so you can get some work done?

Figuring out which conversations you need to have and how to have them is time better spent than worrying about these conversations. You might be surprised at how willing people are to help you and give you what you need. If you don't tell them what you need, are you sure they will know? If it's hard for you to clarify your needs for others, Dr. Rosenberg's (2003) book on nonviolent communication is an excellent how-to guide for learning how to state clearly what is you need and why in a non-confrontational manner.

Another aspect of people-management skills is giving people the benefit of the doubt. When my supervisor and I were frustrated with each other, I went to talk to someone in Graduate Studies about it. What she told me saved the relationship: She told me most supervisors don't derail research, give infuriating answers, and prolong the graduate school process on purpose. If you feel that your supervisor or a committee member has it in for you, you might want to take a step back, remove the emotion of the situation, and give the person the benefit of the doubt. Many professors are responsible for too many classes and too many graduate students.

If you still feel that you are being treated unfairly, talk to someone outside your department for a fresh perspective. That person just might give you exactly what you need to hear to solve the problem and finish your thesis.

⑩ Practice reading management skills.

This tip is particularly for those who are nearer the beginning of their graduate work. The reading load for many graduate students can be overwhelming. Not only is there a lot to read, but some of it can seem impenetrable.

The quantity of reading

One of the things that has really changed about graduate school is the amount of information available. It used to be that you would have your topic, go look in the card catalogue at the library, then pull out a number of books to read. Now you can search through thousands of books and articles online. It used to be that you would be lucky to find enough sources; now you are lucky if you are able to convince yourself that you can stop reading and start writing. If this is difficult for you, remember that you aren't responsible for reading absolutely everything available on your topic. It's impossible.

To get through the readings that you do have, be strategic. An article or a chapter of an edited volume is not intended to be read like a novel. When you read a novel, you start at the beginning and read through to the end. You may skim certain parts and you may skip to the end, but the general idea is that you start at one end and finish at the other. However, when you read an article or a chapter, remember that you don't have to read in order. Start by reading the abstract. If the article seems related to your area of study, read the conclusion. If you want a better sense of what you're reading, your next stop is the discussion. Want to know more? Read the other parts to find out how the study was carried out, what the literature review focuses on, and so on. Use the headings and subheadings to guide you to pull out what you want or need to know from the article or chapter. Cruising through the article's bibliography may give you some good ideas for other things you may want to read on the same topic.

The quality of reading

In addition to reading as much as possible, getting as much out of each reading as possible is important. There are some texts that can be particularly difficult to read. Abstract French philosophy translated into English or a description of complex experiments in opaque jargon can befuddle many readers. In order to understand—and when you pull the article out of your filing cabinet six months later, remember—try these strategies.

Storyboard

This may sound childish, but don't knock it until you've tried it. I used this myself for theory articles when I first started my PhD. I found myself unable to keep track of what the author was arguing and how that argument fit into what other authors argued. To help me process the contents of the article, I started to draw a cartoon of what each theorist was saying; I included with whom they agreed or disagreed, and gave them speech bubbles which summarized in my own way what they were saying through their texts. I should add that I am a shockingly bad drawer, but my stick-people philosophers serve three purposes: one, they helped me keep straight who argued what; two, they help me even now if I need to refresh myself on the various philosophers; and three, they made me, and still make me, laugh. Graduate school doesn't have to be all seriousness. For an example of a storyboard, see the Appendix. It's a storyboard I did up a few years ago to help me deeply understand an article by J. P. Gee (2001) on discourse.

Mind map or timeline

Again, mind maps come in handy when deconstructing a text because you can map out how the ideas fit together. Or, you can use a timeline to discern how an experiment was analyzed. Like storyboards, these visual representations of readings not only engage you deeply in what you are reading, but they serve as quick and easy reminders when preparing for exams or reviewing for your thesis defense.

An annotation system

A piece of text that has been thoroughly read has been written all over. Things you should write on your text include questions you have about the text to later ask your instructor or supervisor and notes regarding how this text connects to other texts you have read. Develop a system that you use on everything you read for graduate school: boxes around key words, circles around the thesis statement and main arguments, new words noted at the top of each page, a summary of the article's main points on the top of the first page, and so on. Once you make a system and stick with it, you'll find it much easier to remember what you've read.

Research journal

Your research journal is an excellent place to write the key points of what you have read. Whether your research journal is hardcover or on your hard drive, consistently summarize what you have read. You can even put your mind maps or timelines in the journal. Add a section for new terms and their meanings. Also, keep track of the questions that came to mind while you were reading.

GRADUATE STUDENT TIP:

What a thesis/dissertation *really* is

It can be helpful to think of your thesis as a training document. You are being guided by your supervisor and committee members to create a document for a certain kind of genre. Consider this to be like a master–apprentice relationship. For this reason, the writing isn't entirely your own; it's being pushed and prodded by others.

The bad news? Your thesis won't be your best piece of writing. After all, you're learning how to write this kind of document for a particular audience. The good news? Your thesis won't be your last piece of writing. You're doing a graduate degree to get somewhere you can't without the certification and skills you'll gain in your program—and it's likely that what you learn from writing your thesis will be directly applicable to your future career.

Of course you'll write up large projects if you are going into academia. Even if you're headed for a career outside of academia, or a hybrid career like academia plus consulting, you'll need to know how to present your research to your audience. This includes:

- Situating your study in the broader context (the literature review and rationale for your thesis),
- Describing the research process (the methodology section),
- Making recommendations (the discussion and limitations sections), and
- Providing a paper trail showing how you got to know what you know (the bibliography).

Think of your thesis not as a document that ends your graduate school life, but one that transitions you to what you'll do after you complete your degree. What skills will you need and how will the thesis-writing process help you gain them? Focusing on why you entered graduate school and what you want to get out of it can lessen your frustration when the thesis-writing process seems to be eroding your soul.

Step 2: Get Focused

Another thing to know is that the thesis isn't and can't be a representation of everything you know. You aren't writing an epic novel. It's fabulous that you've learned so much about your area of interest through your studies, but as I said before, it's easier to write about a narrow topic than a broad one. What you have learned is like a large tapestry. You understand that one thread intersects with another, and that intersection leads to another, and so on. Your study covers a tiny portion of that tapestry: It's like taking a drinking glass and putting it over a small section of the tapestry. The tapestry is large enough to cover a wall—because areas of study blend into one another at their edges—but your study covers just this small circular piece.

How can you possibly write your thesis discussing only this small circle when you know what the rest of the tapestry consists of? We want to share with our readers how this text relates to other texts and areas of study. We can look at our data through multiple lenses, such as a feminist lens or a postmodernist one. What we can write about is endless, but what we *have* to write is not. Your thesis should be a concise, focused document. Your introduction and literature review should set the context of the thesis, but other than that, you have to leave the endless connections and interpretations to the reader. Trust that the reader understands that you know more than what's included in your thesis and can see how your small piece fits into the larger tapestry.

Identify Tasks

STEP 3

Steps 1 and 2 helped you move everything from your mind—the knowledge, the questions, the worries, and so on—onto paper. Before proceeding with the next step, read about the academic writing process. Few graduate students have been explicitly taught how to write academically so it's worth spending some time reading about it now so writing your thesis is as fast and painless as possible.

The Academic Writing Process: 40/20/40

One way to think of the academic writing process is to think of it as broken down into three pieces, into what colleague Susan Doyle and I coined the 40/20/40 split in our writers' guide, *Academic Writing Essentials*. The first of these pieces is planning, and it should take about 40 percent of your writing time. The second piece is writing, and it should take about 20 percent of your writing time. The third piece is revising and editing, and it should take the last 40 percent of your writing time. By dividing the writing process into pieces, you can focus on one piece at a time. Focusing on one piece at a time is a more efficient way to write because you will spend less time revising writing that won't be in your next draft. You also won't be writing before you are ready to write. As Donald M. Murray, the Pulitzer Prize–winning journalist and writing teacher stated, writing too soon is a common mistake among less experienced writers (1985, p.17).

The First 40: Planning Your Writing

Before you begin to write, it's essential to know what you are going to write. The planning stage of your writing can include journaling, free-writing, mind mapping, and outlining. The first two are ways to explore your ideas before you write, and the second two are ways to organize your thoughts so you can begin to write. These methods demonstrate the statement of the famous writing instructor, Peter Elbow, that there are two kinds of writing: One generates words on a page; the other revises those words (1998). Another way of stating the difference is that there is writing to *explore* your ideas, and there is writing to *explain* your ideas. Understanding these two kinds of writing and how they can aid in writing your thesis or dissertation can help you become a more efficient and effective writer.

Free-writing and journaling

Not all writing that we do needs to be "good" writing. Free-writing and journaling are two ways to figure out what you want to say, get in the habit of writing regularly, or explore the connections of ideas and facts. Writing to explore is like doodling with words. You're allowed to make mistakes and go on tangents because it's free-writing. It's what we do to find out what we are thinking or push our thinking further along. I once read an adage that if you can write down in one sentence what's giving you trouble, you are 90 percent of the way to solving that trouble, simply because you can name it. The modern version of this adage is that if you can "tweet" the topic of your thesis or dissertation on Twitter, then you are focused in your writing! (Twitter requires you to state your thoughts in just 140 characters, including spaces). But in order to know what we're thinking, we have to think, and sometimes that involves writing to explore ideas.

Some people consider free-writing and journaling to be the same thing. For me, the best use of journaling is to consider it as a research journal. A research journal is the notebook in which you write questions to ask your supervisor, note call numbers of books to take out of the library, and write about what you are reading—of course, in a free-writing style. A colleague of mine told me that her entire PhD dissertation was written in short, floppy Hilroy notebooks, the kind with the holes down the left side so later you can put them into a binder. She would write the month and year on the cover as she started a new one, and as a result she was able to keep all her notes, thoughts, and activities regarding her writing and research in one place. Since hearing this story, I have switched to Hilroy books myself, for a few additional reasons.

One, the notebooks can fold easily, which means I can carry one with me everywhere. Two, the notebooks are light and made of few pages, which means that I don't feel burdened to carry it around or inconvenienced when trying to find that last note I wrote. Three, they are cheap and ugly. Cheap and ugly aren't usually considered good things, but for research journals, they are the best. Cheap means that they won't break your student budget. Ugly is good because anecdotally I know from working with graduate students that the more special, precious, and beautiful their notebook is, the less likely they are to write in it. Hilroy notebooks are perfect for free-writing, and if you write your grocery list on one of the pages, it's no big deal. But a leather-bound, hand-tooled, grandmother-given notebook might just make you feel that you can write only really fantastic ideas in it. Unfortunately, you may need to write badly to develop these ideas into the fantastic gems they are.

It's through free-writing that these fantastic ideas may emerge. Free-writing can be done anywhere, any time. You can assign yourself a topic before writing, such as the connections between two articles you recently read, or how the findings of a journal article you just finished reading fits into your literature review. The idea is to practice making connections, explaining ideas, and getting in the habit of writing without concern for mistakes. Don't correct spelling or grammatical errors as you write. If you can't come up with the right word, write the wrong word in brackets and keep going. The same is true if you have English as an additional language: Write the word you can't find in English in your first language and worry about the translation later.

Free-writing and journaling can be done anywhere. Use the bits of time you have throughout the day to generate ideas, and sometimes the phrases, that you may need when you draw on your free-writing and journals for the second stage of the writing process. The pre-writing activities that you engage in are not to be pushed into a draft. That can be like pushing a square peg through a round hole. Keep the processes separate, and if you can draw from one to the other, that's lucky, but beware spending time making it work. It might be faster to just rewrite and reword it. It also takes the pressure off writing well when you are free-writing and journaling.

While good writing is grand, it comes in the last stage of writing, that final 40 percent of the writing process. At this point, you're simply using words to explain what you read, what you think about it, and where your research fits with it. You don't need to be in the mood to write. Just get those ideas written down and you can make it beautiful later.

The Middle 20: Writing to Explain Your Ideas

Some academic writing is dense, dry, and convoluted. However, good academic writing is none of these things; instead, it's clear and concise. It weaves together the ideas of others and places your argument, research, or perspective within that weaving. When it comes to the writing that you present to others in the academy, you should already know what you think before you type the first word of your paper. Remember, free-writing and journaling are writing to explore your ideas, while academic writing is writing to explain your ideas to others.

One way to keep this difference in mind is to think that when it comes to academic writing, you must think of your audience. Free-writing and journaling don't have an audience other than yourself. Academic writing has a different audience: other people in the university, including your supervisor, your committee, and your peers. While we like to think that our reader is captivated by our ideas and focused only on reading our words—and clear and concise writing helps with this—it's always a good idea to remember that in this age of multitasking we should really expect that our reader is doing something else while reading. Perhaps they are reading our paper online and, while they are reading it, they are looking at the occasional e-mail that pops into their inbox. Maybe they are texting back and forth with a friend regarding dinner plans. Even if they aren't multitasking, it's our job as the writer to make our writing easy to read. We should expect little from the reader in terms of energy and commitment to reading and a lot from ourselves as writers. Our job as academic writers is to clearly and concisely explain our ideas.

Mapping and Outlining

Mapping and outlining will help you organize your thoughts and materials so that when you're writing you are efficient and effective at explaining your ideas. Mapping refers to concept- or mind-mapping. This is what we did in chapter 1: putting your ideas onto the paper so you can see the connections and decide what to do next. Outlining is what takes you from those steps into the next step in writing, which is figuring out exactly what to write and when to write it.

Take your mind map from chapter 1. Look at the sections on your mind map that you will have to write. Either working on your original mind-map, or from a new version that focuses only on what you have to write at this point in time, add information to it at an even greater level. From your subnodes, or sub-subnodes, add more subnodes until you have each topic or chapter broken down to the paragraph level. Attach the references that you will be using to each node.

For example, Maria can make three main divisions on her map and then order the information into the most logical sequence in which to write it. (Keep in mind that you don't have to write your chapter 1 first; you may decide that you feel more ready to start with your chapter 3). You can see on Maria's map that she has used a system of using capital letters to indicate the major section, numbers to separate the main points in that section, then lower-case letters to organize the subpoints in that section. The subpoints are further organized by roman numerals. Any system is fine as long as you keep it consistent. By dividing and organizing your mind map like this, you should have the information you need to write most of the paragraphs. If your mind map isn't that detailed because you ran out of space, make a new mind map for each section you will write.

So, once a topic is broken down to the paragraph level, you know what the job of each paragraph is, and what information will get that job done. Once you have all your paragraphs of a section mapped out, you are ready to decide the order of the paragraphs in that section. Number each potential paragraph so that it will be clear to you later what you think the order should be. This is your outline. Once you have not only the topic but the contents of each paragraph planned out you'll be able to write each section smoothly and quickly. Some people may prefer at this point to transfer their outline to a Word document so that when they start writing they can simply fill in each paragraph within the outline.

Maria's example

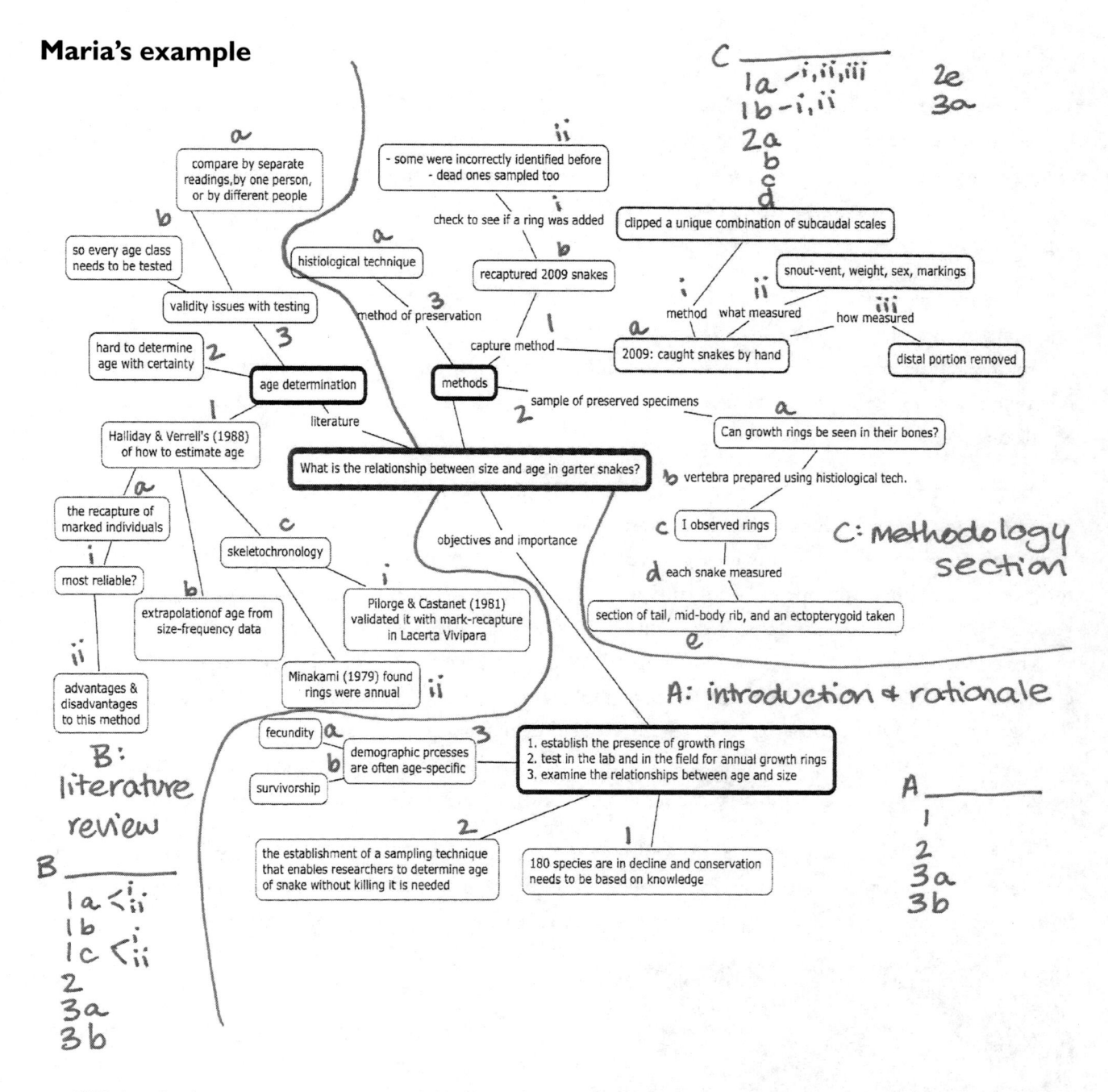

While it's okay to start writing any chapter, it's not okay to start writing any paragraph: Start with the one you labeled as the first. Take out the articles or books you indicated you would need for this paragraph and organize your notes to write the points in the paragraph as you had planned in your mind map or outline. Then, write for yourself the basic structure of the paragraph either on your computer or on a scrap of paper. This structure will remind you of exactly what goes where in this short piece of writing. For example, you can make a paragraph outline like this:

Paragraph #1: Topic sentence_____

   A. first point you are going to make to support the topic sentence
   B. second point to support the topic sentence
   C. third point to support the topic sentence
   D. summarizing or transitioning idea

Managing Your Thesis or Dissertation   29

Remember that one paragraph represents one unit of explanation in academic writing.

Once you know which piece of information or which idea will go first in the paragraph, begin to write. Rather than waiting for inspiration, think of your words as weaving together the information you have already identified, in the order you have already identified it. You know what the job of the paragraph is, and your words will join the ideas and information so that the paragraph will be well organized and clear. As this is only a draft, at this point you don't need to worry about finding the perfect words or overusing certain words.

Because each paragraph is already mapped out and each idea or piece of information is numbered, you can write one paragraph at a time. One paragraph is actually the perfect amount to write at one time: it will take less than one hour to write, and it's easy to commit to. As already mentioned, writing three paragraphs a day is simple if you determine how you can get three forty-five-minute blocks of writing in. One block of writing equals one paragraph.

Here are a few tricks to staying focused. One is to write the paragraph plus the topic sentence of the paragraph you will write during your next writing block. This ensures you have a smooth transition from one paragraph to the next. It also provides you with the hardest part of the next paragraph already written: the topic sentence. When you open your document to start writing the next paragraph, reread the topic sentence you have already written, refer to your map, and write the paragraph. Once the paragraph is done, look at your map to check which paragraph is next and write the topic sentence for that one. Never, ever, reread your previous paragraphs before you start writing the paragraph you're scheduled to write. I promise you, you will dislike what you read and want to tweak it. Rereading your previous paragraph may tempt you to revise before the revisions stage. I strongly recommend that you trust yourself that you did a good job of writing the paragraph because you are so organized and save the rereading—and the revising—for later.

Editing and revising happen after the entire section is drafted. This ensures that when you are in the writing stage you are focused on getting the ideas down on paper. Later, when you revise and edit, you can do it with the entire section and read for flow and overuse of particular sentence patterns and words.

Image © Linnea, 2011. Used under license from Shutterstock, Inc.

The Final 40: Revision

Learning to self-edit can be tricky, but there are some methods that can help you. To revise well, work from a printed version of your work. The first time you read through it, focus on the most important question: Are the ideas clearly explained? By starting with the most important issues, you won't waste time fixing smaller errors in sentences that may get entirely deleted. After you are sure the ideas are clearly expressed, and the order of your paragraphs is logical, you can focus on what the paragraphs are like. Highlight the topic sentence of each paragraph, and check that each sentence in a paragraph supports that topic sentence. Try reading the sentences aloud. Are they very long? Long sentences can be beautifully constructed

30   Step 3: Identify Tasks

but difficult for the reader. The final chapter of this book provides more information on the Final 40 so that when it's time, you can revise, edit, and proofread to improve your draft.

Project Management Concept #3: Identifying the tasks

Now that you know about the two kinds of writing that can help you write your thesis or dissertation—writing to explore and writing to explain—you can keep that knowledge in mind while you do the next task. In project management, the next step after making a thorough mind map of what your thesis or dissertation is about, or the stage of the process you are at, is to identify what needs to be done. Your mind map shows you what you know, and now you will make notes on your mind map about what you have to do. Here are some questions to guide you.

- What conversations do you need to have?
- What information do you need to know, e.g., the length of a proposal in your discipline, or how to get a software program for your data analysis?
- What do you not yet know and need to figure out, e.g., how to carry out your research methodology or how to get ethics approval?

You might want to use sticky notes to add these tasks to your mind map. Focus on identifying all the tasks, big and small, long-term and short-term. Also look at your Worry and Question Boxes; identify what you need to do to address those questions and concerns. For your Worry Box, you may need to think of the conversations you need to have. For example, some students may need to explain to loved ones regarding their need for quiet time in the evenings to write. Other students need to talk to their supervisors to attempt to arrange a better balance of research done for the supervisors and research done for their own studies. The questions in the Question Box can be labeled according to whom you will address them.

On the next page is Maria's task identification list. Instead of using sticky notes, Maria has opted to make a task-identification list while looking at her mind map. She has kept in mind some of the time management and writing process tips included here.

> **Maria's Task Identification List**
>
> - Ask supervisor how long I should expect him to take to give me feedback on each chapter or section.
> - Look up the theses that others have done in this area to gain general information, such as the average page count or length of bibliography.
> - Decide what the limitations to my study might be.
> - Figure out how I can graduate by the end of the year.
> - Decide how to write the methods section. Should I tell it like a story? If so, how can I make it sound academic and scientific?
> - Make a daily schedule that includes writing and reading.
> - Ask my supervisor if I'm allowed to use an editor for the final draft.
> - Make an outline of the next section I'm writing: the literature review.
> - Talk to my friends about my temporary disconnection in the afternoons.
> - Ask supervisor how to balance the answer to "so what?" with an academic voice so the conclusion (introduction?) doesn't sound journalistic.
> - Write the methods section first, then the literature review.
> - Make an outline for the methods section.
> - Think about the journal that I might publish this in. I'd like to have an audience bigger than my defense committee and to produce a document that will help me in my job search.

GET GOING

After you have identified all the tasks you need to do, look at the list on the next page. In the column titled "tasks," write the tasks you have identified. The order doesn't matter. Try to make each item on the list very specific. If the item requires two steps, then it should be two separate tasks. However, the item can be ongoing and broad, such as "read more journal articles" or "write chapter 2." Don't feel like you need to use all the lines in the chart. If you feel confident that you can't break the task down any further and your list is, therefore, complete, then you are ready to move on to the next chapter. However, don't write anything else in the rest of the chart just yet.

Take a look at Maria's example on the next page to see an example. Following that example is a blank chart for you to fill in. Aim for 10 to 14 items on this to-do list. Don't fill in any other column at this point.

Extra charts can be found at the back of the book in the Appendix.

Maria's example

Tasks								
Ask supervisor how long feedback takes								
Look up other theses as examples								
Plan the limitations section								
Make a timeline to know what I have to do to graduate by December								
Decide how to write the methods section; answer my questions								
Make a daily schedule to balance reading and writing								
Ask my supervisor if I can use an editor for my final draft								
Make an outline so I can write the literature review section								
Ask my supervisor and read published theses re: tone of intro & conclusion								
Make an outline for the methods section so I can write it								
Write the methods section								
Write the literature review section								
Browse journals. How can I strategically angle my thesis for publication?								
Talk to my friends about being unavailable in the afternoons								

	Tasks										

GRADUATE STUDENT TIP:

Are you a *nouveau* graduate student?

The French word *nouveau* means "new," and here I'm using it to mean "a new kind." Are you a new kind of graduate student? To answer that question you should know that in the past many graduate students used to study full time. They didn't work except part time as a teaching assistant or research assistant for their department. They often had great funding, cheap rent, and a guaranteed job when they finished.

Some graduate students nowadays are *nouveau*. While others receive great scholarships and research grants that allow them to focus solely on their studies, many others have commitments like a family to raise or parents to look after, a mortgage to pay, or a business to run. As times have changed, so have graduate students. Yet, institutions, departments, and programs may not have adjusted to meet the needs of this new kind of graduate student.

To have some of your needs as a graduate student better met, you may require conversations with your supervisor and committee members to share what your expectations are of them and to understand their expectations of you. These conversations will allow you to explain your circumstances and make clear what a reasonable workload is for you.

Other topics for discussion include what constitutes good writing in your discipline. If you have changed disciplines between degrees or are simply unsure of what writing at the graduate level should be like, talk to your supervisor or a course instructor about it. Your department's graduate advisor and your university's writing centre can also help you to understand the hallmarks of good academic writing.

If you're writing your thesis in a language that isn't your first, or native, language, you may need to make it clear to your instructors and supervisor that you need more time to complete your assignments—both writing and reading—and that you need more guidance to understand the expectations of writing well in your discipline. While some professors already know this from working with previous graduate students working in their second language, some don't and may need to be explicitly asked for guidance. It's worth bringing up your particular needs early on in your studies. One way to frame this conversation is to describe how you think an academic paper is structured. Does your instructor agree? You might ask the instructor to comment on an early draft to ensure that you are on the right track. After all, you are transitioning from one academic culture to another and most of us could use a tour guide when we're in a new place.

Another way you may be *nouveau* is if you're doing your degree online. Studying when you're free and in your own location is fabulous, but you compromise other things, such as easy access to long discussions with your supervisor and the moral support of colleagues. For many students, this compromise is acceptable and even preferable, given their circumstances. Completing the coursework component of the degree can be relatively easy because you are kept to a timeline and there's an instructor guiding you. However, once you finish your coursework it's easy to lose touch with your colleagues and with your own thesis. While this is true for all graduate students, it can be particularly isolating for those who are already physically isolated from the university. To overcome and even prevent this feeling of isolation, join or set up an online writing group or support group to provide you with the people contact you will need to keep going.

While you as a *nouveau* graduate student are definitely smart enough to finish your program, you may not have the other supports in place to help you through it. Take a look at the final chapter to read more about what resources may be available to you.

Image © brushingup, 2011. Used under license from Shutterstock, Inc.

Organize Your Tasks

STEP 4

Project Management Principle #4: Creating the WBS

Creating the Work Breakdown Structure (WBS) means you analyze and then organize your tasks.

Take a look now at the to-do list you have created on the previous page. Which tasks are ongoing (e.g., reading articles or writing a section of your thesis) and need to be scheduled over a period of time? Which tasks are one-off tasks (e.g., sending an e-mail to your supervisor)? Next decide which tasks should happen earlier and which should happen later. A task to be done later may be revising your writing for clarity and concision. If you'd like, make notes next to each item in your list to remind yourself of what sort of task you think each is.

By deciding what tasks you have to do, which should come before others, and the duration of each task, you are deciding how the work will get broken down and spread out over time. Another idea is to assess what tasks are complementary. For example, does reading articles balance nicely with editing a previous section of writing? We are preparing to create a sort of timeline with our list, so we need to be aware of what each task will consist of, and what it will require of you. There's one more step, though, before we schedule the tasks.

Project Management Principle #5: Identifying the Critical Path

Before we can decide what tasks will get done when, we need to know if there are some things that must happen before others, and which tasks can't be tackled until other tasks have been completed. For example, you can't recruit participants for your interview study until you receive approval from your university's ethics board. In turn, you can't receive ethics approval until you submit your ethics application. You can't write your ethics application until you clearly know what your study is about and what questions you will ask your participants.

The critical path defines the core progress of your research and writing. The critical path comprises the tasks that must be done in a certain order or at a certain time. Identifying the critical path facilitates your understanding of the order in which tasks need to be approached. Recognizing the critical path allows you to focus on a handful of tasks at a time. A lengthy to-do list that isn't organized won't reduce your stress level or save you time.

Look at your list of tasks and note which ones must occur before others. Pay attention to things such as grant, award, or ethics applications and their deadlines. While grant and award applications may not have a direct role in your thesis, they can play a supporting role by providing you with funding to live a bit better while carrying out your studies. Winning awards and grants is also an integral part to building your academic CV if you plan to have a career in academia, obtain a postdoc position, or pursue another graduate degree on completion of this degree. As a part of your graduate student life, they may need to be a part of your to-do list. Pay careful attention to dates; you'll need letters of support from people like your supervisor, your past supervisor, a colleague, and so on. The more time you can give them to write the letter, the better.

Just as award and grant applications may play a role in your graduate work, so might your ethics application. If you plan to conduct research on people, animals, or biological parts of either, you need to complete an ethics application. An ethics application form is lengthy and asks you to describe your study from many angles. If you are working with people, the form asks you how you will recruit participants, what degree of anonymity you can provide to them, and how you will store the data. If you are working with animals, the form ensures that you are aware of the regulations designed for the ethical and humane treatment of your research subjects.

When I was doing my PhD, ethics applications took six to eight weeks to be read, and it was common for students to be asked to make revisions to their applications to ensure that the highest standard of ethical treatment of people and/or animals was being met. Ask around your university or call the Ethics Office to ask what usual processing times are for both the initial application and the revisions. Add two weeks to that so you won't be scrambling to deal with last-minute changes to the planned timeline of your study.

Image © alegria, 2011. Used under license from Shutterstock, Inc.

Develop Task Understanding

Generally, you will want to understand which of your tasks:

- Must occur before or after another task on the list (the critical path)
- Are ongoing tasks, such as writing
- Are one-off tasks, such as sending an e-mail to update your supervisor on your progress
- Are in your control (because of your amazing self-discipline)
- Aren't in your control (because you can't control people and processes)
- Need to broken into smaller pieces

Some tasks, such as waiting to receive feedback on a chapter from your supervisor or committee member, are not in your control. Rather than sitting and waiting, though, you can fill that time with other tasks that don't require that feedback. Other tasks, on reflection, encompass too much or are vague; these need to be broken into subtasks.

Look at how Maria's tasks, taken from her chart from Step 3, can be understood in terms of timing and control.

- *Ask supervisor how long feedback takes*
  This one should be done first so that she can determine the best order of tasks. She isn't in control of how long the feedback will take but by asking her supervisor what she can expect she will be able to build the wait time into her timeline.
- *Look up other theses as examples*
  When this task happens isn't so important. A task like this is a good one to do when you have heavy-thinking tasks like reading and writing going on.
- *Plan the limitations section*
  Planning is important as Maria can't write the limitations section until she has an outline or plan for it. However, she has other sections to write as well so this task could come later.
- *Make a timeline to know what I have to do to graduate by December*
  A task like should be done sooner rather than later in case making the timeline reveals a step she has missed. If there's a firm deadline, all planning should be made not only forward to that date, but backwards as well. It's surprising how many little steps there are after submitting the thesis to the committee. Consulting guidelines regarding when documents have to be in to your university's Graduate Studies Department is integral to finishing by a specific date.
- *Decide how to write the methods section; answer my questions*
  This will be a task that occurs over a few days or weeks. Deciding on the approach to a section will lead to knowing how it will be organized, which in turn leads to planning it out and then writing it.
- *Make a daily schedule to balance reading and writing*
  Here's a task that should come first because it dictates how Maria can accomplish her tasks. Balancing the tasks between heavy and light thinking and between one-off and ongoing tasks keep the process of working on the thesis interesting and achievable.
- *Ask my supervisor if I can use an editor for my final draft*
  This is a one-off task that can come later. Maria is not close to her final draft, but this question is important because the answer will indicate to her how much effort and time she may need to put in to cleaning up the final copy. In addition, Maria is writing her thesis in English, which is her second language. This adds an extra layer of worry for her because she has to focus on using the most appropriate words and correct grammar. If departmental rules dictate that she isn't allowed to use an editor for the final draft, she may want to ask her supervisor for a special concession because she's writing in her second language. (Personally I've always felt that if you can write a good thesis in your second language, you should be awarded *two* degrees.)
- *Make an outline so I can write the literature review section*
  Because she has an advanced mind map, Maria is ready to write a number of sections, including the literature review. An outline will help her know what to write in each part of the literature review to simplify—and expedite—the writing process. This task should be done sooner rather than later.

- *Ask my supervisor and read published theses re: tone of intro & conclusion*
  Tone is an interesting topic and one that requires some analysis. This task can come at any point in the WBS.
- *Make an outline for the methods section so I can write it*
  Like the outline for the literature review section, Maria needs to make it before she can write the section. Maria should plan each section with her mind map first and then focus on planning the contents of each section one at a time. This will help her stay immersed in one section while knowing how all the sections will fit together.
- *Write the methods section*
  Of course, this task happens after the section is planned and should be planned over a number of days or weeks.
- *Write the literature review section*
  (same as above)
- *Browse journals. How can I strategically angle my thesis for publication?*
  Keeping an eye on publication is strategic. As postdocs become the new PhDs, the race to develop your academic CV now starts while you are still in graduate school. The thesis can be publishable on its own, but remember that many journals don't accept articles longer than twenty-five pages. Maria can think about turning her thesis into a book, a website, or a series of articles. Knowing what the articles in the journals are talking about and how they are talking about those topics will help Maria know how she might best angle her chapters or her eventual articles. As well, keeping in mind a greater goal of publishing what she's writing may help her stay motivated when she's feeling overwhelmed. Because Maria doesn't intend to stay in academia but instead get a professional job, angling her thesis to facilitate this transition is strategic.
- *Talk to my friends about being unavailable in the afternoons*
  This task may take some thought because it requires delicacy. It can be hard on friends and family to feel shut out, even if it's just for a few hours a day. This is especially true given how connected people are through text, social network sites, and e-mail. This task needs to come earlier rather than later so that Maria has the best chance of sticking to her tasks and timeline.

Jiro's tasks are clearer once he has reduced the scope of his study. As noted earlier, he's a single parent and a part-time worker. Scheduling in time management strategies are especially important to him. Also, because his goal is a tenure-track position, Jiro wants to make habits now that allow him to write, research, and read in a way that's balanced with the other roles he plays in his life. He may also want to investigate universities to determine where he might want to eventually apply and what areas of research those faculties are involved in.

GET GOING

Analyze the nature of each task you identified in the chart in Step 3. The critical path—or the order in which certain tasks need to be done—should become clear to you. As well, you should have a clear understanding of which tasks need to be rewritten to better demonstrate the steps involved in them. You'll draw on this task analysis to build your timeline in the next chapter.

GRADUATE STUDENT TIP:

Are you demonstrating academic integrity?

Academic integrity is one of those things that people seem to talk about like a parent chiding a child: Don't cheat! However, having academic integrity means more than not cheating; it means knowing the rules of the university when writing about the ideas, research, theories, and findings of others.

In graduate school you read a lot. Reading widely in your field of study informs you of the main ideas and findings that are important to what it is you want to study. Knowing more about your subject means you know what other people wrote about it. Because your ideas are built on or situated in the context of the ideas of others, you need to make reference to what ideas or findings come from where. This is called citing your sources.

Your university's website will have some useful guidelines about how to cite sources. The general rule is that you need to note in the body of the text what your sources are, and you need to repeat that information with more detail at the end of your text in a references or bibliography section. This creates a paper trail so that an interested reader can easily find the source you are referring to. It also shows the reader how you came to know what you now know. By demonstrating this to your reader, you are demonstrating academic integrity.

There are three common errors graduate students make when it comes to academic integrity. The first is bad paraphrasing. Paraphrasing is a difficult skill to master because so few of us have been taught to do it well. A good paraphrase of a quotation requires you to use your own words to capture the meaning of the quotation. You can't simply replace a few words and call it your own writing. If you don't change enough of the quotation and there aren't quotation marks around it, technically that is plagiarism.

The second error is called patch writing (Howard, 1999). When you take chunks of text from another source and input it directly into your writing, then you are not really writing with your own words. Of course, academic writing requires you to call on the words of others, but most of the time you should paraphrase those words. Save quotations for the really well said or the impossible to paraphrase. Your paper shouldn't be a quilt of different people's words, sewn together with a few of your phrases. An example is having in your literature review section a paragraph starting with "Brown (2004) argues that" followed by a long quotation, followed by another paragraph starting with the same pattern and another long quotation from a different article. The patches in this example belong to someone else. Your job when you write your literature review is to interpret the findings and apply them to your research context, not to provide the highlights of each article in the authors' own words. Because you are producing a text that has more words belonging to others than to you, you are violating the rules of academic integrity, even though you use quotation marks. It's the ratio of your words to the words of others that matters.

The third error is hiring an editor, rewriter, or translator without having the prior permission of your supervisor. Each university and each department within your university will have its own perspective on this topic. Some departments will encourage you to hire an editor. Other departments see the involvement of another person in your writing as a violation of academic integrity because it is no longer your own work. Be sure that your hard work isn't jeopardized by not following the rules.

In addition, academic integrity means protecting your work from being used by others. The clear example is if you lend your work to others so they can get credit for it. Less clear is when you don't protect your work from being copied without your knowledge or permission. Having your words taken from you may be worse than you think. What if someone took your writing and published it? Both would cause serious problems when it comes to defending your work in front of your committee. After all, the hallmark of a thesis is that it's original work. If someone else uses what you wrote before you publish it in your thesis, it's not yours and therefore not original.

Working ethically with your human participants also requires maintaining the standards of academic integrity. What if keeping your files easy to access (or easy to cut and paste, if you keep a public blog or post pieces of your writing on a social media site) jeopardizes the anonymity you promised to your research participants? You have a duty to maintain their dignity and the level of anonymity you promised them—and that includes gossiping about participants or sharing their words in ways other than you indicated on your ethics application form.

Generally, you can ensure you are demonstrating academic integrity by following these principles:

- when in doubt, cite,
- paraphrase well,
- protect your writing,
- protect the writings, ideas, and findings of others, and,
- ask if you can hire someone to help you with your writing. It doesn't hurt to ask.

Image © Icons Jewelry, 2011. Used under license from Shutterstock, Inc.

Make a Plan

STEP 5

Project Management Principle #6: The Gantt chart

The Gantt chart is a special kind of chart. You can see in Maria's example, pages 47 and 48, that she has added time to the top of her chart. She has also used her task analysis and understanding to fill in the chart to indicate which tasks must be done when, in which order, and how long she predicts each will take.

GET GOING

Your tasks are listed down the left side; now, across the top you will write down periods of time. Looking at your tasks, choose time periods that suit your tasks. Some suggestions are:

- months
- two-week periods (e.g., March 1st–14th)
- weeks
- two-or-three day chunks (e.g., Monday to Wednesday, Thursday and Friday)
- days of the week

Decide on time spans that are reasonable for you. Keep in mind what other responsibilities you have, such as work and childcare. If you have a vacation or family responsibilities coming up, don't schedule that time in your the Gantt chart, or schedule fewer tasks for that time period.

Take a pencil, pen, marker, or pencil crayon. Shade when you will do each task. Some tasks will have just one time period shaded, while others will have multiple periods shaded. For example, sending an e-mail is a one-off task, so you will shade just one box. Writing a chapter, however, will likely require you to shade multiple boxes. Aim for a balance of tasks so that you aren't doing all the mental heavy lifting at once; you might find a periodic check of new literature a good counterbalance to writing the next section of your results.

Things to keep in mind:

- Balance your tasks in kind and length. Try to have a few tasks to do each time period.
- Pay attention to the critical path.
- Be kind to yourself by expecting an appropriate amount of high-quality work.
- Ensure your success by scheduling your success. Don't set yourself up to fail. Being a graduate student is hard enough without creating extra opportunities to feel bad and even more stressed out.
- Make sure you are in a constant state of work rather than having busy times and less busy times. While you are waiting for one thing, like data to come in, you should be doing something else for your thesis, like checking on new literature or writing your methods section.

A Gantt chart can provide a great deal of relief for graduate students who get stressed over the amount of work they have to do. Feeling stressed? Simply fold the chart over so you can see only the tasks that you have to do today. The whole list can be overwhelming; if you've organized your Gantt chart well, you should be able to breathe easier when you look at only what you have to do today. Trust yourself that your timeline and tasks are good; follow through with what you have planned.

Image © Icons Jewelry, 2011. Used under license from Shutterstock, Inc.

Maria's example

Tasks	Dec 27–31	Jan 1–15	Jan 16–31	Feb 1–15	Feb 16–28	Mar 1–15	Mar 16–31	Apr 1–15	Apr 16–30
Ask supervisor how long feedback takes		■							
Look up other theses as examples			■		■				
Plan the limitations section						■			
Make a timeline to know what I have to do to graduate by December	■								
Decide how to write the methods section; answer my questions			■						
Make a daily schedule to balance reading and writing	■								
Ask my supervisor if I can use an editor for my final draft									■
Make an outline so I can write the literature review section			■		■				
Ask my supervisor and read published theses re: tone of intro & conclusion							■	■	
Make an outline for the methods section so I can write it				■					
Write the methods section				■	■	■			
Write the literature review section			■						
Browse journals. How can I strategically angle my thesis for publication?							■	■	
Talk to my friends about being unavailable in the afternoons	■								

Managing Your Thesis or Dissertation 47

GRADUATE STUDENT TIP:

Take Control of Feedback

One of the strangest things about universities is that professors are sometimes hired for their research capabilities over their teaching abilities. Even those who demonstrate excellence in teaching can be unaware of how to design writing assignments, design tests, and provide useful feedback on written work. The one that affects graduate students writing their theses the most is the quality and quantity of feedback they receive on their drafts.

Quantity of Feedback

Bear in mind that the easiest thing to do is find fault with a piece of writing. When I look at a piece of graduate student writing, I can see dozens of things that I would have done differently. Of course, I am a different person with a different writing style. I am also a trained writing instructor. Your supervisor is in a similar position because she or he has read many thesis chapters and has more subject knowledge than you. Part of my training as a writing instructor has been to learn to limit the kind and amount of feedback that I give at any one time. Unfortunately, many professors think the other ways—lots of feedback on lots of things, or nothing but praise—are preferable. They are wrong.

Too much feedback

When you receive a lot of feedback on your writing, it can be hard to work your way through it all. Even though you know better than to take it personally and to over-identify with your writing, it can be hard on your self-esteem. One of the best ways to approach this kind of feedback on your chapters is to read bits of it at a time. Choose times when you feel strong and able to detach yourself from the feedback. Try making a list of the feedback on a separate piece of paper so that you are doing something physical, rather than emotional, with the feedback. You can later address the feedback by using your list as a checklist. A template of feedback has been included in the Appendix for you to try.

Step 5: Make a Plan

As you go through your list you'll notice that some of the feedback addresses global concerns, such as the organization of a section or the use of a theory in analyzing data. These global concerns are the ones that require your immediate attention. By changing a significant aspect of your writing you will likely need time, more thought, and another draft of your document. The more local concerns are things like grammar, citations, added references, and so on. These require time as well, but less thought because they are less important to the overall document. Do the big stuff first and focus on the smaller stuff later.

When looking at your checklist of feedback, remember that just because something was suggested doesn't mean you have to follow it. If you feel strongly dissatisfied about something your supervisor has suggested, discuss the suggestion with her or him. Likewise, remember that you aren't going to be the sole creator of this document you are writing, so it's okay if pieces of it aren't exactly as you would have it. In my own dissertation I added a theory and a handful of references that a committee member wanted in it. The issue I had with this was that I was totally unaware of them until I read her feedback. However, I added them. The result was a stronger document, but one that didn't represent only my ideas. If I was writing a book or a piece of poetry, this might have been unacceptable to me, but because a dissertation is a training document, I was able to suck it up, add the pieces, and move on so that I could finish my degree. I could imagine those people who were patiently waiting for me to finish—coworkers, family, partner, and staff—silently cheering my decision to move forward rather than put up a fight.

Too little feedback

Some students get little feedback because their supervisors have little to give. This situation arises when the piece of writing is so good that there is little to suggest or when the supervisor doesn't feel confident in his or her ability to deconstruct a piece of writing. You have two options here. One is to ask for feedback on specific aspects of your writing, such as its organization or readability. You could ask him

Image © brushingup, 2011. Used under license from Shutterstock, Inc.

Managing Your Thesis or Dissertation

or her to draw a red line under any sentence or part of the writing that was difficult to read or otherwise confusing. These red lines will indicate where you need to focus when you are revising your writing. The second option is to seek writing advice elsewhere, such as at your university's writing centre, a graduate student writing group, or a private academic writing coach. Again, it's always best to ask for specific suggestions so that you get specific feedback.

Quality of feedback

Just as the amount of feedback can be problematic, so can the quality of it.

Mean feedback

If the feedback is particularly venomous, mean-spirited, or just plain unkind, the best thing to do is remember that people are generally uncomfortable with and untrained at providing constructive criticism. Criticism on its own is easy, but being constructive and kind is difficult for many. Instead of feeling hurt, try to reframe your reactions to feeling sorry for the person who wrote it because obviously they are uncomfortable providing feedback, most likely because on some level they recognize their inability to do it well. If you have that rare supervisor who is mean and enjoys tromping on the souls of his or her graduate students, then take heart: You can read the feedback knowing that the vindictive quality to it is merely a representation of the personality of the person who wrote it. It does not necessarily reflect the quality of your writing.

In short, ignore the disrespectful tone or unkind words and dig deeper to find the gems of writing wisdom that they are covering. No matter how mean or bad at giving feedback your supervisor is, he or she probably knows a great deal more about academic writing in your discipline than you do. Also, supervisors don't plan to destroy graduate students because doing so would reflect badly on them. Personalities and egos might make for a bumpy graduate ride but most supervisors want their graduate students to complete their degrees. Detach yourself emotionally from the feedback and make a list of the constructive aspects it provides.

Slow feedback

Perhaps one of the most vexing forms of feedback is that which is slow to arrive. This can be most inconvenient when you have your Gantt chart to follow. My advice is to allow for lots of time to receive the feedback when you first plan your chart, but once a pattern of lateness has been demonstrated by the committee member or supervisor, allow for an even greater delay in your timeline. Polite e-mail reminders and a phone call or two may be in order, but unfortunately there's little we can do to change the nature or busy schedule of others.

Other quality issues

There are other issues regarding the quality of feedback. If you don't understand the feedback because it's illegible or unintelligible, you need to ask about it. Another situation is when one committee member makes one suggestion and another makes a conflicting suggestion. When this occurs, your first task is to inform your supervisor, because your supervisor is the one with the final say over your thesis.

Control the feedback

In addition to removing the mean-spiritedness out of feedback and reining in unruly and copious feedback, you can control feedback by using it to improve your writing not just on this piece but on future pieces of writing.

Once you have received and applied feedback, you may start to notice a pattern to it. When revising my own writing, I was surprised to discover that I was a flagrant ignorer of comma splice rules and that my tone was rather dogmatic. Revising alone didn't catch these errors. My supervisor pointed them out to me on my first draft, my second draft, and, embarrassingly, on my third draft. I then caught on to my pattern of errors and was able to fix them before subjecting my supervisor to them yet again. When you get certain feedback repeatedly, you are provided with a learning opportunity to improve your writing and self-editing skills. Take it.

Follow Your Plan

STEP 6

Following your plan requires that you trust your plan is a good one and if it isn't, you'll make a better one. It also requires a stepping back from your thesis. Identifying yourself with your thesis is an easy way to make yourself crazy, rather than getting your thesis done.

Project Management Principle #7: Ownership

A thesis or dissertation is not you nor is it a representation of all you know. Instead, it's a training document, as explained in the first Graduate Student Tip. Because your committee will have some say in how the document is shaped and written, it is best to accept you don't have control over it. According to project management principles, the project manager doesn't own the project itself. Likewise, you don't own the thesis. Rather than making you sad or feeling like the process isn't yours, think of it as liberating. Because it's a training document, and because it's not only yours, it's okay that it isn't perfect. You should have a big say in the process and the outcome of your thesis, but yours isn't the only say.

Letting go of ownership of the outcome can help you accept a thesis that is less than perfect. Even if you think it's perfect, I promise you that in five or ten years you will reread it and find it cute. It will be cute because since you finished writing it you have read more, researched more, and learned more. The finished thesis or dissertation represents what you did, read, and knew at that particular time in your life. As soon as the thesis is complete, it becomes a historical document of your graduate student research and writing. You are not your thesis, just as your thesis is not you.

If we tried to write the perfect thesis, we would never finish it. There will always be new articles to include in your bibliography and new information to add to your literature review. It's hard to restrain ourselves from writing about connections to other ideas, research, and areas of study, but we have to. The dissertation or thesis must be limited or it will be an epic novel, not a graduate school document.

Project management principle #8: Use your resources

Identifying the resources available to you can help you succeed. After all, your writing isn't built on your ideas alone—hence the need for citations—so why should your graduate experience not rely on the help of others?

Subject librarian

Your subject librarian can show you how to have a reasonable return on your database searches so you don't have to sift through hundreds of hits.

Committee members

Your committee members are on your committee for a reason; each one has expertise in a particular subject and/or methodology relevant to your study. Ask them questions to help guide your research and your writing.

Image © Icons Jewelry, 2011. Used under license from Shutterstock, Inc.

A university writing centre

At the writing centre you can ask a tutor to help you with common writing issues, such as wordiness or with citations. Bring feedback from previous papers or questions about what you are currently writing to guide your sessions. While a tutor can't read your entire thesis, a tutor can help you become a better writer by looking at sections of it. For both the rest of your thesis and beyond, becoming a better, faster, more confident writer is a good thing.

A writing group

If there isn't one already running in your discipline, your colleagues might be interested in forming a writing group with you. Whether you meet in person or communicate online, it's helpful to read the writing of your peers. There are some aspects of writing your colleagues will be better at than you; there will be some aspects that you are better at than they. You can learn from what they do better and you can feel good about what you are already doing well. The size of group I recommend is four to six members.

There are two main types of writing groups. The first is when you give feedback on each other's writing. With your colleagues, decide on the amount of feedback you will give each other. Will it be detailed, or will you indicate the sentences and sections you found difficult to read? Either is fine, but everyone should provide the same amount of feedback. One of the biggest benefits of this kind of writing group is that as you read the writing of other students to help improve it, you strengthen your ability to read your own writing to improve it. Practicing reading for understanding versus skimming over the ideas you already know so well may transfer well to your own self-editing skill set. More information about self-editing is in the final graduate student tip, next.

The second style of writing group is one that agrees to write together: The members write at an agreed time and check in with each other's progress. One group I know meets every Tuesday to write in each other's company. While there's some laughter (and a lot of coffee!), there's also a lot of writing. This style of writing group may serve particularly well students who feel disconnected from their university and cohort and/or those who need cheerleading and human contact more than they need editing.

Ombudsperson or Graduate Studies Department personnel

Both Graduate Studies and your university's ombudsperson are great resources to talk to when you feel that communication with your supervisor or committee members has broken down. They keep your conversation confidential, provide you with strategies to strengthen your strained relationship, and guide you through some of the finer points of university regulations, policy issues, and rules of academic integrity.

GET GOING

Take some time to identify what resources you haven't used that might make the writing and research process easier or more enjoyable. Take some time, too, to practice an emotional detachment from your thesis. Bear in mind that the best thesis is a finished thesis, and that five years from now it won't matter that you got a certain section completely right; what will matter is that you finished your thesis. Imagine yourself taking a physical step back from your writing. If that's difficult for you, try making a list of what other skills you are learning or practicing while writing your thesis. For example, you will be a better researcher and a stronger critical reader. You will have worked on your people skills to interact with your committee members. And your ability to manage your time and a large, long-term project will be improved. Knowing what benefits your thesis can bring you and your résumé will help you keep the thesis contextualized as a way of learning.

If the thesis currently sits in your mind as an obstacle, then you may not be able to overcome it. If the thesis sits in your mind as a way of accomplishing something—getting a graduate degree, a better job, a deeper understanding of what you are studying—then you may be less likely to see this as the title match of you versus your thesis. The thesis is a means of accomplishing something. Although it's an accomplishment in and of itself, what you learn from it through the process of writing it is what matters most.

GRADUATE STUDENT TIP:

Self-editing strategies

Few people have been taught to edit their own writing. Being a graduate student is an excellent time to improve your writing skills because you have a built-in reason for doing so: finishing your thesis. A well-written, clear, and convincing thesis is a good document to bring forward into your next work environment. In addition, solid writing skills—which include self-editing—are an essential skill for whatever that work environment is.

I've compiled this self-editing guide to address graduate students who are writing a thesis (or dissertation or project) and those who are writing a course paper. Once you have written a draft that you are comfortable with, use these activities to tighten your writing, emphasize your arguments, and clarify your descriptions.

At the paper level

- ❏ Take another look at the assignment guidelines. Have you answered all the questions and addressed all the aspects the guidelines specify?
- ❏ Highlight the paper's thesis statement. Is it strong? Is it clear? Is it out front where the reader can't miss it, or have you hidden it? Remember, some writing styles put the thesis statement last so that the entire paper leads up to it. That's fine in other kinds of writing, but in academic writing in Canada and the United States you want to have your thesis statement early on. The reader should know what your paper is about (the context), your reason for writing it (the argument), and how the paper is organized to support the reason for writing it. This last point refers to the "map" you give readers. It can be as simple as "This paper will provide an overview of the literature then situate my research in that context to demonstrate why the results of the experiment disprove the commonly accepted theory of learning." In this sentence the writer has laid out the path of the paper: overview of literature, followed by a description of how the research fits into that literature, and then a discussion of the meaning or importance of the research results. Readers of academic writing in the United States and Canada generally expect writing to tell them what the piece is about and how it will be organized—and they like to be reminded periodically throughout the piece through

subheadings or sentences that reiterate what has been discussed and how it links to what's coming up next.
❏ Go through and highlight all terms and jargon (if you are allowed to use jargon). Have you provided the reader with a definition of each one? While you may think your reader will know the terms and jargon, it's necessary to explain exactly how you are using them.

At the section level

❏ Highlight the thesis statement of the section, or the sentence that frames what the section is about, if you can. If you can't find one statement, you probably need to add one to the introductory part of the section. This statement tells the reader what your writing is going to do, so don't hide it. Make it easy for the reader to find it.
❏ On a separate sheet of paper, write down the topic sentences of each paragraph. If a paragraph doesn't have a topic sentence, give it one. What is the job of each paragraph? How does it support, explain, or expand on the thesis statement of the section? You should end up with a nice alignment between the thesis statement of the section and the paragraphs' topic sentences. This activity ensures that your argument is clearly supported by evidence and examples. While you are at it, think about how your paper or section is organized. What other ways could it be organized? Do any of those ways make more sense? Would your writing be smoother if you reorganized the sections or paragraphs?

At the paragraph level

❏ Each paragraph needs a topic sentence. The topic sentence tells the reader what the job of that particular paragraph is in relation to the thesis statement of the section or the entire paper. What is the topic sentence of each paragraph? Does every sentence in the paragraph relate to that topic sentence? Does each sentence belong in that particular paragraph, or would some of them be better in a different paragraph under a different topic sentence?
❏ Direct quotations may provide solid evidence for your argument, but they can make your writing clunky. To improve the flow of your writing, turn many of your direct quotations into paraphrases. Paraphrases capture the meaning of the quotation but use your own words. Note that changing just a few of the words (like *the* to *a* or *come*

to an agreement to *agree*) doesn't make a paraphrase. Some direct quotations are too difficult to paraphrase and therefore should be left as is. Others are just so well said that it seems important to include them and they can be left as is. Be aware of block quotations, though, because they sometimes contain information or arguments that distract the reader from what you want them to focus on. Be strategic in your use of quotations, and remember that it's your job as the writer to introduce every quotation. Don't expect the reader to guess at what you want them to understand from it.

❏ Check for repetition. Our first drafts can be full of repetition because we're allowed to write badly so we get all our ideas out on the paper. When we self-edit we cut out the repetition. Look for sentences that don't align with the paragraph's topic sentence; the sentence may need to be moved or deleted. Look at each paragraph's job. Is each clearly different from the others? If not, can the sentences be put in other paragraphs or does the paragraph need to be refocused or deleted?

❏ Take your list of paragraph jobs from the "At the section level." In that list you specified what each paragraph was about and how each one supported, developed, or explained the thesis statement. Check now that each sentence in each paragraph is doing its job to support the overall job of the paragraph. The organization of the paragraph should reflect the job. For example, if a paragraph's job is to define a concept, then each sentence should tackle an aspect of that definition. If the job is to provide an example, the example should be clearly stated, then explored. Most importantly, don't hide your point in the paragraph. Make sure the point of each paragraph—the job—is easy for the reader to identify.

At the citation level

❏ Go through your entire thesis paper and ensure that each quotation or paraphrase is correctly referenced in the text. Look at the page numbers, quotations marks, parentheses, dates, and names; are they correct? Then double-check that every work you refer to in-text is included in the bibliography at the end of the document. If you are a long-term graduate student, be sure that as you move through revisions that you are aware of any changes to the style guide you are expected to use.

At the sentence level

- ❏ Use the spellchecker. If a word comes up as misspelled, and you know it's not, don't worry about it.
- ❏ Use the grammar checker. If a phrase or sentence comes up as questionable, check it out. While your sentence may sound good to you, there may be a better way to say it. Even if you don't want to change it—for example, you want to use the passive voice in that particular sentence—at least you have thought about your choice and are sure of its correctness for the context.
- ❏ To edit at the sentence level, choose paragraphs at random. If you edit by starting at the first paragraph and work in order, then you may end up focusing more on the ideas in your writing rather than on what's actually on the page. Read each paragraph aloud; this is one of the best ways to catch small mistakes. For example, the spellchecker won't pick up that you've typed "hen" instead of "then" or "from" instead of "form."
- ❏ Work on one paragraph at a time. Highlight the subject of a sentence (the main topic being discussed or described, or the person doing something, for example) in one colour and the verb (an action or state, such as *runs, jumps, is, seems*) in another. Strong sentences have the subject and the verb together. If they are separated by a clause, as in the example below, see if you can move the clause so that the subject and verb can be next to each other.

    The research, although preliminary, is revealing.

    In this sentence, *the research* is the subject. *Is* is the verb. *Although preliminary* is the clause separating the subject and the verb. The sentence would be better written with the subject and verb as neighbours:

    Although preliminary, the research is revealing.

- ❏ Circle all the sentences that begin with:

    It is   This is   They are   There are   These are

    These are empty subjects, which means the real subject is hiding somewhere near the end of the sentence. Sometimes it's hard to find a different way to start a sentence, which is fine because I recommend aiming to change about half of the sentences that start with an empty subject. One easy fix if you have written "These are" or "This is" is to add a noun in between the two words. For example, "This study is" and "These ideas are" are clearer than "this is" and "these are" because they remind the reader what the subject is.

It would be great if we could all write our first draft with few empty subjects but it's difficult to do so. Reading all that academic writing can lead us into some pretty bad habits because, sadly, not all academic writing is well written. Some writing seems deliberately dense and puzzle-like. Therefore, I recommend writing your early drafts using all the empty subjects you want since you know you will fix them later. You can't do everything at once.

- Try to put the verb near the beginning of the sentence. If you hide the verb at the end of the sentence, the reader has a lot to keep straight about the subject before finding out what that subject is doing. It's your job as the writer to make your meanings clear. Don't ask your reader to do your job for you; make your writing easy to understand.

Here's an example.

The participants of the focus group, which was held in June after the initial interviews, discussed the topic of poverty in Canada.

In this sentence the verb, *discussed*, comes near the end of the sentence. The reader has a ways to go in the sentence before she or he knows what the subject of the sentence is doing, is like, etc. The verb could be moved closer to the beginning:

After initial interviews, participants discussed the topic of poverty in Canada in a focus group.

- Circle all the sentences that have *is* or *are* as the main verb of the sentence. This verb—to be—is common, but it's also weak. Can you substitute stronger verbs in some of these sentences?
- Some sentences should be long, some should be medium length, and some should be short. When we look at examples of academic writing, long and complex sentences seem to be the norm. However, just because you see long sentences in academic writing doesn't mean you need to emulate that. The trend now is for clearer and crisper writing. This style of writing appeals to more audiences and communicates information more easily, which arguably is the point of academic writing in the first place.

Use a variety of sentence lengths to spice up your writing. Short sentences are punchy and focus the reader on your point. Long sentences allow you, for example, to incorporate the ideas of others in a nice paraphrase. Medium-length sentences serve as the balance for the two.

❏ Eliminate unnecessary words; they make your sentences wordier than they need to be. Look at the following three categories and see if you tend to use any of them. If you do, they are likely places where unnecessary words are impeding clarity.

1. Taking the long way to say something:

   make a decision can be *decide,* *come to an agreement* can be *agree.*

2. Saying the same thing twice:

   return back   *past history*   *period in time*   *share in common*

3. Using adverbs and adjectives when you don't need to:

   actually   *kind of*   *definitely*   *totally*

❏ Check to see if you have used any clichés. A cliché is a standard set of words that's commonly known. If I said the first half of the cliché, it's likely that you can finish the cliché for me. While a cliché may pop up here and there in your early drafts of academic writing, be sure to prune them from your final draft to ensure that your writing is fresh and less predictable.

   in this day and age → *nowadays*

   tried and true → *reliable*

   since the beginning of time → *for a very long time*

   without a doubt → *likely*

❏ Avoid casual language. In academic writing we don't use language that we would use when speaking casually with our friends. Sometimes casual language takes the form of clichés. Another example is the use of contractions. Contractions join two words together in common combinations, such as *isn't, don't,* and *can't.* In academic writing you can't use contractions. Also avoid expressions like "Now we're going to talk about the research findings." That sounds like you are speaking to your audience in a presentation, but a spoken presentation, not a written one. Writing is different than speaking.

Managing Your Thesis or Dissertation

❏ Restrict the number of rhetorical questions you use. Rhetorical questions are questions that you "ask" the reader but they aren't really questions because you aren't waiting for the reader to respond before moving on. They're used to make the reader think about the topic and become a bit more engaged with the text. A rhetorical question used here and there in your paper is a nice change from all those nonquestions you have written, but too many of them—either throughout your paper or all in a row in the introduction—will make the reader think you are just listing questions. How will the reader know which question is the most important? How will the reader know what you plan to do with all these questions? As demonstrated here, two in a row is the limit; if there are more, your sprinkling of questions becomes more of a shower.

At the punctuation level

Here are some common errors to look for in your writing.

❏ **The Comma Splice**

Do you have a comma before the word *and*? It's okay if you are using that combination in a list

apples, bananas, and oranges

but it's not okay if you have a full sentence after the comma and are using *and* to introduce it

Recent studies suggest breast cancer may be linked to air pollution, and these findings need consideration if we are to prevent this disease.

Rather than join the two sentences with a comma and *and*, which creates the error of a comma splice, the two sentences should be separated or joined in another way.

Recent studies suggest breast cancer may be linked to air pollution. These findings need consideration if we are to prevent the disease.

OR

Since recent studies suggest breast cancer may be linked to air pollution, consideration of these results can help prevent the disease.

❏ **Misused Semi-Colons**

There are two specific occasions on which a semi-colon can be used. The first is to join two short sentences with a similar or the same subject. On each side of the semi-colon must be a full sentence, which means that the sentence has a subject and a verb.

Graduate students need to be aware of publishing opportunities; résumé development is important for entry or re-entry into the job market.

The applications of the research findings are varied and numerous; an outline of these applications will be given in the following section.

In both examples, the topic is either similar or the same. In the first example, publications lead to a stronger job application package. In the second example, the research findings are the focus of both sentences before and after the semi-colon.

So why join sentences at all? Why not just avoid the semi-colon altogether? The answer is for variety and style. When you have two short sentences in a row with a similar topic, you can join them to make a fancy sentence. You can leave them, but that puts two sentences of the same type one after the other. As short sentences are used for punch and focus in academic writing, the reader may be left wondering why you've chosen to give him/her a double punch with this particular information.

The other instance is when you are providing your reader with a list of items which in themselves contain commas. If you were to use commas to separate the items on the list, you'd confuse the reader. That's why we use semi-colons in this instance instead of commas.

There were three participants in my pilot study: Melanie, a preschool teacher; Juan, a college biology instructor; and André, a high-school counselor.

The findings demonstrate two correlations: age, years of work experience, and extrinsic motivation; and attitude toward program and intrinsic motivation.

❏ **Misused Colons**

Colons can be used in a number of circumstances, but in academic writing I recommend using it in two situations. One is preceding a list if what comes before the colon is a full sentence.

There were three research questions I wanted to answer:

1. How can I better support instructors to design more effective writing assignments?

2. *How do instructors view their current writing assignments? What do they perceive to be the strengths and weaknesses of these assignments?*

3. *How do the instructors evaluate these current assignments, and why? Are they satisfied with their evaluation systems?*

Another instance in which a colon is used in academic writing is when you have the combination of a full sentence, followed by a colon, after which comes a further definition of the first full sentence. Some examples to help clarify this are:

There was one issue all the participants raised: the difficulty of doing group projects.

The intriguing answers to the survey led me to another research question: Why were many of the respondents indicating a dislike of their unit manager?

The first example shows the pattern of "I'm telling you something" plus "and this is exactly what it is." Another common, but non-academic, example is:

There is one thing I love truly and passionately: chocolate.

Again, the first sentence introduces the framework, and then what follows the colon is what's inside that framework. The second example, regarding the survey answers, follows this pattern, as well, because how the new research question is arrived at is the framework for what that new question is. The difference between that one and the preceding example is that the first one doesn't have a full sentence after the colon while the second one does (in this case, in the form of a question). If you use a full sentence, capitalize the first letter. Other examples to demonstrate the second pattern are:

One question continues to stymy supervisors of graduate students: Why does it take these students so long to finish their theses?

The focus group session elicited much data useful to understanding our research question: We learned how teenagers view their parents' use of alcohol.

Strategies to develop your self-editing skills

❏ Use the checklist at the back of this book to go through one item at a time. With practice you will get faster at each item. Once you get the hang of each activity, use this checklist to keep you on track.

- Switch papers with someone in your discipline. When you read someone's paper, it's better than yours in some ways, and not as good in others. Identify what those ways are and learn from them. For example, does that writer use smooth transitions between sections or paragraphs? Maybe you can learn how to do that by identifying exactly how that smoothness is created. Or, perhaps that writer uses long, complicated sentences that you find difficult to understand with one reading; remember that long sentences can have that effect on the reader when you are self-editing.
- Always self-edit on hard copy. Print out one copy and edit it at every level; then go and change it on the computer to make the next draft.
- Always read aloud from your hard copy. When you read aloud you catch sentences that sound awkward. You can also correct many of the small grammatical errors and typos you make.

References

Maria's mind map is based on:

Waye, H. L. (1992). *Age determination of individual garter snakes (<u>thamnophis</u> spp.) using skelentochronology* (Master's thesis). University of Victoria, Victoria, BC.

Jiro's mind map is based on:

Waye, H. L. (2010). *Learning how to work with instructors of international EAL graduate students to better support their students' development of academic writing skills* (Doctoral dissertation). University of Victoria, Victoria, BC.

Burke, K. (1967). *The philosophy of literary form: Studies in symbolic action,* 2nd ed. Baton Rouge, LA: Louisiana State University Press.

Carnegie, D. (1981). *How to Win Friends and Influence People.* New York: Simon & Schuster, Inc.

Elbow, P. (1998). *Writing With Power: Techniques for Mastering the Writing Process.* New York: Oxford University Press.

Gee, J. P. (2001). Quality, science, and the lifeworld: The alignment of business and education. In *Difference, Silence, and Textual Practice: Studies in Critical Literacy,* pp. 359–362. New York: Hampton Press, Inc.

Graff, G. & Birkenstein, C. (2006). *They Say, I Say: The Moves That Matter in Academic Writing.* New York: W. W. Norton & Co.

Howard, R. M. (1999). *Standing in the Shadow of Giants: Plagiarists, Authors, Collaborators.* Stamford, CT: Ablex Publishing.

Murray, D. M. (1985). *A Writer Teaches Writing,* 2nd ed. Boston: Houghton Mifflin Co.

Rosenberg, M. B. (2003). *Nonviolent Communication: A Language of Life,* 2nd ed. Encinitas, CA: PuddleDancer Press.

University of Victoria, Department of English. (2010). *Academic Writing Essentials*. Toronto: Pearson.

University of Victoria, Human Resources Department. (2008). *Project Management*. Workshops. June, 2008.

Appendix

Extra mind map pages 70
Extra Gantt chart pages 86
Gee (2001) storyboard 91
Feedback chart 92
Self-editing checklist 95

The Worry Box

The Question Box

The Worry Box

The Question Box

The Worry Box

The Question Box

The Worry Box

Appendix

The Question Box

The Worry Box

The Question Box

The Worry Box

The Question Box

The Worry Box

Appendix

The Question Box

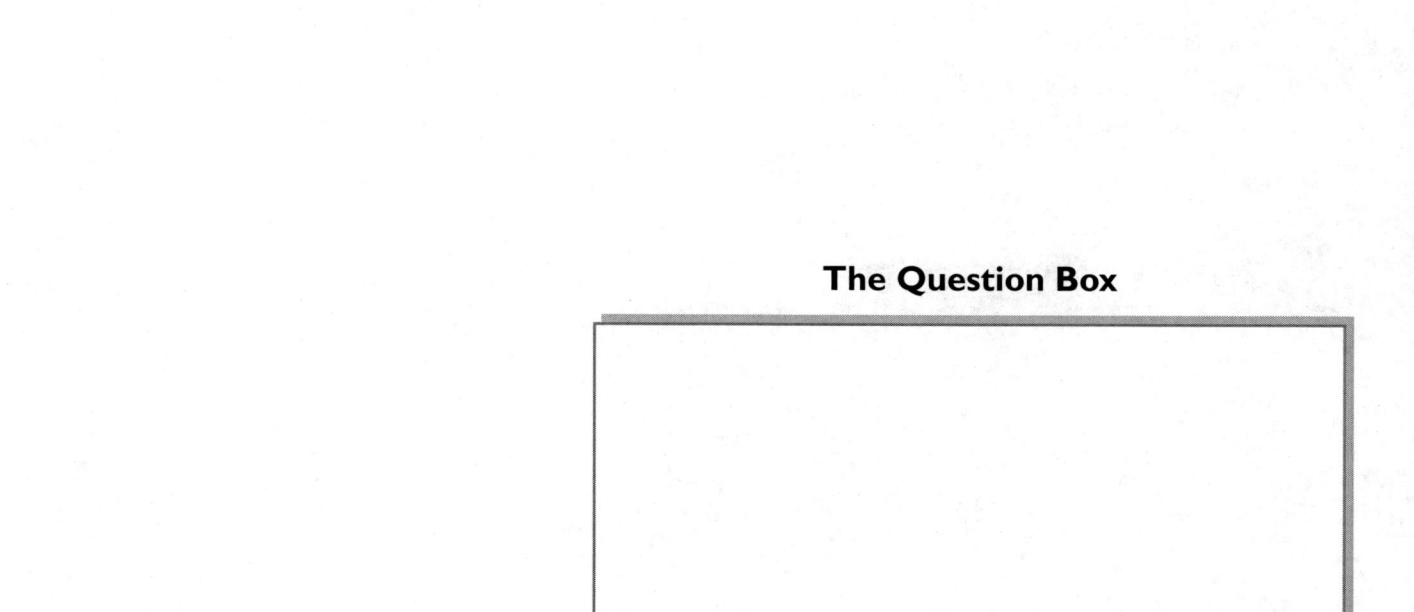

The Worry Box

The Question Box

	Tasks									

Tasks									

Tasks

Tasks									

Tasks									

A Drawing of Gee's (2001) Quality, Science, and the Lifeworld: The Alignment of Business and Education

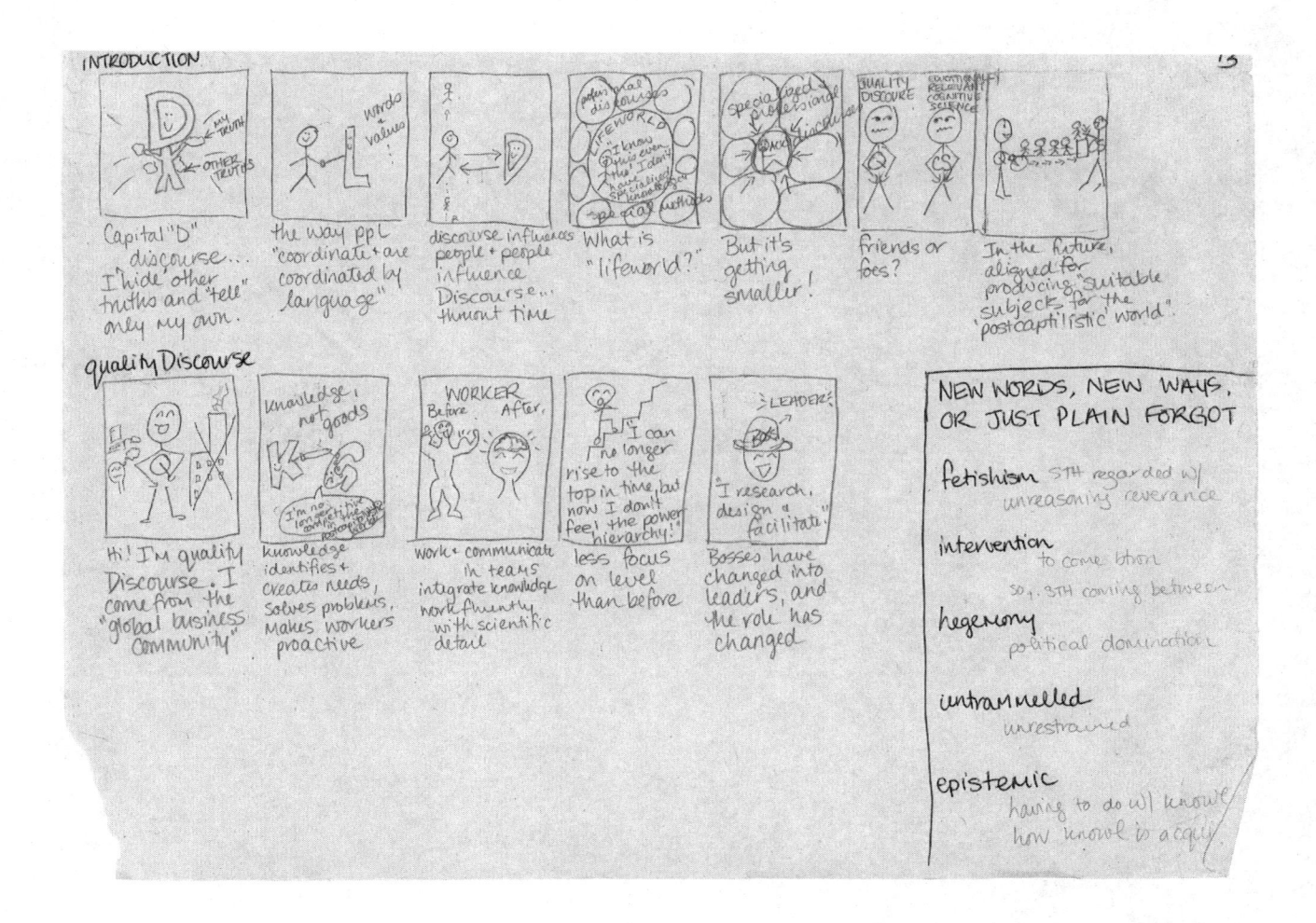

This is the first of three pages I created a storyboard for. There are two sections of the article I covered on this page, the introduction and Gee's definition of quality discourse. As I read the article, I drew, erased, and redrew as my understanding of his arguments became clearer to me. You can also see that I keep a vocabulary box on the first page. When I started my PhD I was surprised at how many words I didn't know, or if I thought I knew them, they weren't being used according to the definition that I knew. Keeping the cartoon and the vocabulary list made it easier for me to quickly review articles and increase my understanding of disciplinary terminology.

Managing Your Thesis or Dissertation

Feedback Chart

Write what you have been asked to add, change, or address. Then put an X in the appropriate column to indicate whether it's a global concern (big) or a local concern (small). An example of a global concern is a misunderstanding you have of a theory you used to underpin your research that your supervisor has just pointed out in your draft. Global concerns require you to think about the feedback, analyze what you have written, and make changes to at least one sentence and likely to much more than that. Examples of local concerns include grammatical mistakes, requests for added references, and unclear sentences Global concerns need to be addressed before local ones.

Suggestion or request	Global?	Local?

Suggestion or request	Global?	Local?

Suggestion or request	Global?	Local?

Self-Editing Checklist

❏ Does your writing fulfill the assignment criteria or objectives you have for this section?

❏ Where is the thesis statement?

❏ Have you provided a one-sentence outline or map of how your paper or this section of the paper is organized?

❏ Have you defined all the terms so the reader knows how you are using them?

❏ Does each paragraph have a topic sentence?

❏ Make a post-outline of the job of each paragraph and how the paragraphs support your thesis statement.

❏ Choose a paragraph and reread all the sentences it contains. Do all the sentences relate specifically and clearly to the topic sentence?

❏ Do you have a good balance of direct quotations and paraphrases? Have you used block quotations appropriately?

❏ Are your direct quotations accurate?

❏ Does your paper feel repetitious? Highlight the parts that do and see if you can hone your text so it doesn't seem as repetitious.

❏ Is the point of each paragraph clear to the reader? How do I know?

❏ Have you used the style common for your discipline? Have you paid attention to how this style lays out headings and the references section?

❏ Have you used the spellchecker function on your draft?

❏ Have you used the grammar checker function on your draft?

❏ Have you read your paper aloud to find grammatical mistakes, typos, and awkward phrasing?

❏ In most sentences, are the subject and verb neighbours?

❏ Have you circled all the sentences that begin with empty subjects?

❏ In most sentences, is the main verb—the one indicating the action in the sentence—near the beginning of the sentence or it more often hidden at the end?

- ❏ Have you used strong verbs in most of the sentences?

- ❏ Does your writing have a variety of sentence lengths?

- ❏ Have you checked your writing for wordiness?

- ❏ Have you checked your writing for clichés?

- ❏ Have you used the voice of a writer communicating with a reader, as opposed to the voice of a speaker communicating with a listener? Have you avoided casual language?

- ❏ Have you used only a few, if any, rhetorical questions?

- ❏ Does your writing contain any comma splices?

- ❏ Have you used the semi-colon correctly?

- ❏ Have you used the colon correctly?

- ❏ Have you reread your writing to predict the feedback you would receive on this current draft? What changes should you make?